Nina Boudreault

BOOKS BY JOHN HOLLANDER

Poetry

Tesserae and Other Poems   1993
Selected Poetry   1993
Harp Lake   1988
In Time and Place   1986
Powers of Thirteen   1983
Blue Wine and Other Poems   1979
Spectral Emanations: New and Selected Poems   1978
Reflections on Espionage   1976
Tales Told of the Fathers   1975
The Head of the Bed   1974
Town and Country Matters   1972
The Night Mirror   1971
Types of Shape   1969
Visions from the Ramble   1965
Movie-Going   1962
A Crackling of Thorns   1958

Criticism

Melodious Guile   1988
     Fictive Pattern in Poetic Language
Rhyme's Reason   1981
     A Guide to English Verse
The Figure of Echo   1981
     A Mode of Allusion in Milton and After
Vision and Resonance   1975
     Two Senses of Poetic Form
The Untuning of the Sky   1961
     Ideas of Music in English Poetry 1500–1700

For Children

The Immense Parade on Supererogation Day
     and What Happened to It   1972
The Quest of the Gole   1966

Selected Poetry

SELECTED POETRY

BY
JOHN
HOLLANDER

Alfred A Knopf New York 1993

THIS IS A BORZOI BOOK
PUBLISHED BY ALFRED A. KNOPF, INC.

Poems from the following collections are used by permission of
The Johns Hopkins University Press

Blue Wine, copyright © 1979 by John Hollander
In Time and Place, copyright © 1986 by The Johns Hopkins University Press

The remaining poems in this collection were originally published in the following books:

A Crackling of Thorns, copyright © 1958 by Yale University Press
Movie-Going and Other Poems, copyright © 1962 by John Hollander
Visions from the Ramble, copyright © 1965 by John Hollander
The Night Mirror, copyright © 1971 by John Hollander
Town and Country Matters, copyright © 1972 by John Hollander
Tales Told of the Fathers, copyright © 1975 by John Hollander
Spectral Emanations, copyright © 1978 by John Hollander
Powers of Thirteen, copyright © 1983 by John Hollander
Harp Lake, copyright © 1988 by John Hollander

Library of Congress Cataloging-in-Publication Data

Hollander, John.
   [Poems. Selections]
   Selected poetry / John Hollander.
      p.   cm.
   ISBN 0-679-41931-4
   I. Title.
   PS3515.03485A6 1993   92-54789
   811'.54—dc20   CIP

Manufactured in the United States of America
First Edition

Again, for Harry and Kathleen

CONTENTS

FROM TALES TOLD OF THE FATHERS (1975)

FROM TOWN AND COUNTRY MATTERS (1972)

FROM THE NIGHT MIRROR (1971)

Notes on many of the poems will be found beginning on page 333

From Harp Lake

KINNERET

As the dry, red sun set we sat and watched
  Them bring the fish in from the harp-shaped lake.
At night my life, whose every task is botched,
  Dreams of far distant places, by mistake.

They tunnelled through the mountains to connect
  The raging ocean with the inland sea.
Dreaming of you, I wander through some wrecked
  Historic region of antiquity.

We played unknowing for the highest stakes
  All day, then lost when night was "drawing nigh."
The dark pale of surrounding hemlocks makes
  Stabs at transcendence in the evening sky.

Out on the lake at night one understands
  How the far shore's more distant than a star.
The music playing right into my hands,
  I took the measure of my dark guitar.

Beauty? the dolphins leap. But for the truth,
  The filtering balein of the great whale.
Age? it's more gullible than flashing youth:
  The ending swallows the beginning's tale.

Far from the freeway and its hoarse, sick roaring,
  He can still listen to the wildwood's sigh.
Across the world the shattering rain was pouring:
  Tears merely glistened in my childhood's eye.

Out of the depths I call for you: the water
  Drowns it, as if that sound were its own name.
Enisled in height, she learned what had been taught her:
  From closer up, the sky was more of the same.

Her thought was silent, but the darkness rang
    With the strong questions of a headlight's beam.
He walked around the lake: the water sang
    An undersong as if it were a stream.

The wind was working on the laughing waves,
    Washing a shore that was not wholly land.
I give life to dead letters: from their graves
    Come leaping even X and ampersand.

Below, the dialect of the market-place,
    All dark *o*'s, narrowed *i*'s and widened *e*'s.
Above, through a low gate, this silent space:
    The whitened tomb of wise Maimonides.

Only a *y*, stupidly questioning,
    Separates what is yours from what is ours.
Only mute aspiration now can sing
    Our few brief moments into endless hours.

The merest puddle by the lowest hill
    Answers the flashing sunlight none the less.
I harp on the two flowing themes of still
    Water and jagged disconnectedness.

I lay in a long field; eleven sheep
    Leapt from a barge onto the grass, and fed.
She cleared the wall and leapt into my sleep,
    Riding her piebald mare of night and dread.

Dressed like their foes, nomadic and unkempt,
    The emperor's legion crept across the stream.
Only as her great rival could she attempt
    The soft parapets of her lover's dream.

The voice of the Commander rang in us;
   Our hearts in stony ranks echoed his shout.
The cold, bare hills have no cause to discuss
   What the thunder among them is about.

Musing at sundown, I recall the long
   Voyages across shoreless seas of sand.
Shuddering at dawn, I call out for your song,
   O isle of water in the broad main of land.

What speck of dust fell on my page of strife
   And mixed its coughing with the prose of breath?
The pensive comma, hanging on to life?
   The full stop that sentences us to death.

From his blue tomb the young sun rises·and
   The marble whitecaps pass like dancing stones.
A boy, somewhere in an old, arid land,
   Sat carving spoons out of his father's bones.

Windward, the sun; a galley on our lee
   Rolls gently homeward; now its sail is gone.
This miracle the moonlight once gave me:
   The sky lay still; the broad water walked on.

What cannot be seen in us as we stare
   At the same stretch of ordinary bay?
Her constant dreaming of the Immermeer,
   My half-lost moment on the Harfensee.

In bright, chaste sunlight only forms are seen:
   Off-color language gives the world its hue.
Only in English does the grass grow green;
   In ancient Greece the dogs were almost blue.

The bitten-into fig does, without doubt,
  Show forth that blushing part of which we've heard.
Resemblance turns our language inside-out:
  Pudenda is a self-descriptive word.

He fought Sloth in her arbitrary den,
  And grew bored long before he could defeat her.
I stop—something is too pedestrian
  About the iambs in this kind of meter.

Footsore, his argument gave out and slept
  In the unmeasured vale of meditation.
In marked but quiet waves the water kept
  Time with the heartbeats of an old elation.

This night in which all pages are the same
  Black: the Hegelians must shut up shop.
It seemed when, smiling, you called out my name
  The humor of the noon would never stop.

He parsed his schoolboy Greek, the future more
  Vivid, where rich, strange verbs display emotion.
My glass of dark wine drained, from the dim shore
  I scan the surface of a sparse, gray ocean.

They built beside a chilly mountain lake
  The prison of particularity.
The sun is blind now; only the stars awake
  To see the whole world mirrored in the sea.

The sea's a mere mirror wherein you see
  Something of the gray face of the high sky.
Far from shore, the dark lake relays to me
  The lie of the old, silent land nearby.

The everlastingness of childhood's summer
   Evenings itself skyrockets and is gone.
As if great age would evermore become her
   The far-lit winter night reigns on and on.

Snows on the far, long mountain in the north,
   Seen from the lake, are never reflected there.
Gazing at distance, I keep setting forth
   Unwittingly into the thoughtless air.

We stand our ungiving ground, our unpaid mission
   To creep through fields or scamper across the town.
Still at last, supine, we learn what position
   Earth took on the great issues of up and down.

A kingfisher flashed by them on their lee
   To lead their thoughts toward a blue yet once more.
My tears blur world and water and I see
   Each seed of flickering lake, each drop of shore.

The dry, unsinging river that runs south:
   Somewhere along it we must some day cross.
The memory of music in my mouth
   Sticks to my silence now like leaves, like moss.

Some husbandman will plow where now I row;
   My lively wake will be the long dead road.
Drowning our songs, the river will flood and go
   Mad, as if flowing were itself a goad.

My mind's eye, wearied of distrust, soon turned
   To surfaces, of which it then grew fond.
She meditated on the mud that churned
   Up from the fruitful bottom of the pond.

Down in undreaming deeps the heavy carp
  Fed, while above the shining surface trembled.
Was it my voice that spoke for the bright harp?
  Or was it a heart the singing lake resembled?

Some say I mutter; some, that I reconditely
  Shout: but meanings, like words, like air, expand.
Some fragments hurt you when you grasp them tightly,
  Some feel as if they were part of your hand.

Every dog has his day, and the worm turns
  Nasty within the hard, absorbing grave.
The heat of August threatens as it burns
  Our hearts with the dead cold of winter's cave.

The wind turned to the hard hills and wondered
  At their cold heads and then began to hum.
My white and faulty mortar should not have sundered
  Under the grinding of this cardamom.

Pale cliffs descend below the sea and steep
  In the full silence, calm and unconfounded.
He broke through the thrumming surface of his sleep
  As if some lake-shaped instrument had sounded.

THE MAD POTTER

Now at the turn of the year this coil of clay
Bites its own tail: a New Year starts to choke
On the old one's ragged end. I bite my tongue
As the end of me—of my rope of stuff and nonsense
(The nonsense held, it was the stuff that broke),
Of bones and light, of levity and crime,
Of reddish clay and hope—still bides its time.

» «

Each of my pots is quite unusable,
Even for contemplating as an object
Of gross unuse. In its own mode of being
Useless, though, each of them remains unique,
Subject to nothing, and themselves unseeing,
Stronger by virtue of what makes them weak.

» «

I pound at all my clay. I pound the air.
This senseless lump, slapped into something like
Something, sits bound around by my despair.
For even as the great Creator's free
Hand shapes the forms of life, so—what? This pot,
Unhollowed solid, too full of itself,
Runneth over with incapacity.
I put it with the others on the shelf.

» «

These tiny cups will each provide one sip
Of what's inside them, aphoristic prose
Unwilling, like full arguments, to make
Its points, then join them in extended lines
Like long draughts from the bowl of a deep lake.
The honey of knowledge, like my milky slip,
Firms slowly up against what merely flows.

» «

Some of my older pieces bore inscriptions
That told a story only when you'd learned
How not to read them: LIVE reverted to EVIL,
EROS kept running backwards into SORE.
Their words, all fired up for truth, got burned.
I'll not write on weak vessels any more.

» «

My juvenilia? I gave them names
In those days: Hans was all handles and no spout;
Bernie believed the whole world turned about
Himself alone; Sadie was close to James
(But Herman touched her bottom when he could);
Paul fell to pieces; Peter wore away
To nothing; Len was never any good;
Alf was a flat, random pancake, May
An opened blossom; Bud was an ash-tray.
Even their names break off, though: Whatsisface,
That death-mask of Desire, and—you know!—
The smaller version of that (Oh, what was it?—
You know . . .) All of my pots now have to go
By number only. Which is no disgrace.

» «

Begin with being—in an anagram
Of unending—conclude in some dark den;
This is no matter. What I've been, I am:
What I will be is what I make of all
This clay, this moment. Now begin again . . .
Poured out of emptiness, drop by slow drop,
I start up at the quarreling sounds of water.
Pots cry out silently at me to stop.

» «

II

What are we like? A barrelfull of this
Oozy wet substance, shadow-crammed, whose smudges
Of darkness lurk within but rise to kiss
The fingers that disturb the gentle edges
Of their bland world of shapelessness and bliss.

» «

The half-formed cup cries out in agony,
The lump of clay suffers a silent pain.
I heard the cup, though, full of feeling, say
"O clay be true, O clay keep constant to
Your need to take, again and once again,
This pounding from your mad creator who
Only stops hurting when he's hurting you."

» «

What will I then have left behind me? Over
The years I have originated some
Glazes that wear away at what they cover
And weep for what they never can become.
My Deadware, widely imitated; blue
Skyware of an amazing lightness; tired
Hopeware that I abandoned for my own
Good reasons; Hereware; Thereware; ware that grew
Weary of everything that earth desired;
Hellware that dances while it's being fired,
Noware that vanishes while being thrown.

» «

Appearing to be silly, wisdom survives
Like tribes of superseded gods who go
Hiding in caves of triviality
From which they laughingly control our lives.
So with my useless pots: safe from the blow
Of carelessness, or outrage at their flaws,
They brave time's lion and his smashing paws.

—All of which tempts intelligence to call
Pure uselessness one more commodity.
The Good-for-Nothing once became our Hero,
But images of him, laid-back, carelessly
Laughing, were upright statues after all.
From straight above, each cup adds up to zero.

» «

Clay to clay: Soon I shall indeed become
Dumb as these solid cups of hardened mud
(Dull *terra cruda* colored like our blood);
Meanwhile the slap and thump of palm and thumb
On wet mis-shapenness begins to hum
With meaning that was silent for so long.
The words of my wheel's turning come to ring
Truer than Truth itself does, my great *Ding
Dong-an-sich* that echoes everything
(Against it even lovely bells ring wrong):
Its whole voice gathers up the purest parts
Of all our speech, the vowels of the earth,
The aspirations of our hopeful hearts
Or the prophetic sibillance of song.

Powers of Thirteen

For Natalie Charkow

I
_____

This is neither the time nor the place for singing of
Great persons, wide places, noble things—high times, in short;
Of knights and of days' errands to the supermarket;
Of spectres, appearances and disappearances;
Of quests for the nature of the quest, let alone for
Where or when the quest would start. You are the wrong person
To ask me for a circus of incident, to play
Old out-of-tunes on a puffing new calliope,
Or to be the unamused client of history.
But tell me of the world your word has kept between us;
I do what I am told, and tell what is done to me,
Making but one promise safely hedged in the Poets'
Paradox: *I shall say "what was never said before."*

Refusing to Tell Tales

2
_____

Late risers, we sleep through all the morning's heroics,
The triumphant winds of early light that blow the last
Rags of dark to pieces and sweep them away, the fierce
Levée of the flaring monarch of our globe. We give
All that high stuff the runaround, getting up in broad
Customary stretches of appearance, breakfasting
In the midst of things that have been going on awhile.
Thus we need not undergo the old delusion that
Comes from entering the day soon after all the great
Goings on, feeling that morning has been warmed by our
Work. Thus we need not add our own weariness to that
Of afternoon; and as far as endings are concerned,
One does not begin feasting at dawn, but at sundown.

None Too Soon

3

So we came at last to meet, after the lights were out,
At someone's house or other, in a room whose ceiling
Light was accidentally switched off—and there you were
In a corner where I had not seen you just before
When I had rushed in looking for someone else. Even
Then the shadow of an earlier time deepened the
Room—and this was before I learned that in my childhood
You lived across the alley-way, the light of your room
Crept through my window-blinds, throwing ladders of light up
My ceiling in the dark (when I was four I thought that
"Shadows" meant spills of illumination from without).
Then, years later, I stumbled upon you, standing next
To an unlit floor lamp, against a mute looking-glass.

The Shadow

4

At the various times of the year I have paid you
Plaintive visits, as on mornings when it was too hard
To believe that the fog would be burnt off before noon
By the very sun it hid; or moral ones at high
Midday, when hot shadows of how things seem are barely
There; or towards sundown when, walking up a reddened beach,
Cool shadows of long remembrance convening as one,
(Oh, that there were so much shade at the noon sun's great heat!)
I have headed your way at a recreative time.
But when we walk out at night, or early on some fine
Afternoon, all preliminary colloquies yield
Their various tones to the broad translations of light
And dark, laid on with late strokes, fit for our going forth.

Visiting Hours

5

At first you used to come to me when everything else
Seemed to have gone away somewhere—even those winter
Absences which themselves will desert cold orchards in
The January thaw, before returning the land
To its definitive hardness—and where a few broad
Strokes preserved the momentary pink, scratched at by bare
Trees, of winter twilight. Hedged around by denials
Of scene, we could deem ourselves to be the place we made.
Now, speaking figures of light, we redeem the barren
Plenitudes of picture, even in postcards and views
Crammed with the illustrative, as of the dumb head of
El Capitan at the specious twilight's first gleaming,
Or of lonely Neuschwanstein on its tinhorn summit.

Then and Now

6

Your bright younger sister whom so many fancy to
Be you was always getting in the way when your friends
Were about. An "altogether inconvenient child
With an alarming memory" one of them said once.
She would help you sometimes when a trick was to be played,
A pompous visitor to be derided, something
Lost, or broken, to be covered for; but for the most
Part, she was up to all her own mischief. From her touch
Nothing was safe. But then, what she did was all for show,
Nothing was changed, ongoings of every day outgrew
Her goings-on. But it is your doings that have made
The difference to me; I walk down the boulevard
With you unnoticed: her red hat makes everyone stare.

Fancy-Pants

7

Earth, water, air and fire were not elementary
Enough, after all, for our minds' desire—even though
They covered matter's three phases of solidity,
Flow and spirit, and commingled with them the hot light
Of thought and passion interfused, and made up four good
Candidates for the noble order of foremost things.
But then we multiplied the simplicities, until
The periodic table folded up. Now again
The elements are four: I myself, whose hand and heart
And inner eye are one and indivisible; ink,
Discursive, drying into characters; the hard, white
Ground of this very page; and, for the fourth, yourself: air
In which I burn? Or the fire by which I am consumed?

The Elements

8

Lying in love and feigning far worse (we love to know
That show of pain consumed it and none was left to feel)
For so long we had made up dozens of excuses
—Excuses for making up excuses they were—out
Of the stuff of love. Ah, but even saying it makes
The heart sink: what do we make things out of—need? desire
To have, to make? Or rather out of whole cloth? Or yet
The tattier fabric of vision and oversight,
Undersong humming along with it all, Gretchen's wheel
Spinning its own disco music? This can go on and
On, but what of candor now, of truth? We must reflect
On this obscurity with a bright, open face, not
Foolish, and musingly look at the dark and light up.

The Pretext

18

9

One evening in early spring Father gave us dimes:
George planted his in the hard and sour ground of the yard,
Hannah pasted hers to a card and drew crayoned wings
About it, little Willie lent his to a playground
Friend who never paid him back, and I—I took the dime
And let it lie among other coins in my pocket,
Hearing it jingle, safely hidden away among
The ringing gathering of its own kind, like itself
All unspent and all quite blind to just what being saved
Had meant—loss of glitter in the places of exchange,
Of all the energies of getting and expense. Yet
It could sing out: my dime could rhyme with its own echoes,
Down inside a buried sound it was no death to hide.

Hidden Rhymes

10

The power of "might" that makes us write—the possible
Worlds without you in them that takes so much describing—
Reveals the poverty of what we can never have,
All those echoes, in the dense, thoughtful forests, which can
Never speak their own minds, all those images which would
Have flashed across the faces of our amenable
Mirrors, had the world been otherwise, the want of you
Been part of its unwisdom, as it were. As it is,
Naming you for what you are, taking you at your word,
I have pushed my way through the thickets to the treasure
Of onlyness, of the immense wealth of our one world,
Yet wary of its edge, as where our selves cast, in this
Hidden wood, unkind, black shadows of unlikelihood.

Feigning and Necessity

11

May-day, the day of might, day of possibility
That became the name of cries reaching out for help from
General disaster: it has come and gone again
With all its shows of power—the phallic mayhem round
The village pole; the parading of the red banners;
The branches' payday after weeks of budding, silver
And gold of first blossom yet unspent in the heyday
Of later flowering. Then June will waste her substance
In riotous living, then that auxiliary
Verbiage with which the sociable seasons discourse
Of their own vainglory will parade itself and raise
Ruckus enough for millions of dancing villages,
Scarlet petals enough for all the new worlds in earth.

Aftermath

12

Dahl and Forsyth, Freese and Fuchs, Weigel, Wister and Zinn
Stand about my piece of the land, making it their own,
Chatting along the fence, standing tall at the corner
Of the lot, or clambering up a white column on
The porch to have a look-see into the neighbor's yard.
In a noise of color, spring empties itself into
Summer, rumoring of more, better and worse, to come,
Flowers laughing in the sunlight of their sprightly names.
Earth will write them up in its book of rising accounts
Even as the names of my locals get written out
In their discoveries, their illegitimate get:
Spring-weekend-and-summer people, some regulars, some
Nonce visitors, seem to be taking over the place.

Summer People

In search of a note I half-remember your having
Written me, I went rummaging through the table-drawer
Over by the window. Half-stuck at first, it opened
At a jammed angle and all I could make out inside
Lay in a scattered jumble: blunt, small scissors some child
Had once been given, a matchbook from the old Chambord,
A half-crushed shuttlecock, three dulled pennies, a crescent
Inchlong moon from a jigsaw puzzle with cutout shapes
Hidden in it (part of a mirror in the picture).
The tales of their entrances into the drawer are not
Your story or mine; but what they were doing for years
In the dark, preparing their piece of astonishment,
Is just the matter of our quiet conspiracies.

Half-Opened

I am preparing a perpetual calendar
Out of what might have been mere journals (a page a day,
False confidences, commonplaces commented on,
Perhaps a pressed wildflower here and there, all of which
I find will not do for you) and some half-printed leaves
Torn from copies of the Farmer's Almanac in years
When it had been quite wrong about the winter's weather.
(Counting the days till, say, next August the whatever
Has never been your way, who have always made them count.)
There is a season for every time, and thus I rule
Boxes and fill them with new songs and ongoing jokes,
Not the matter of what merely happens written down
But written up, in this old ledger, the true account.

Never Out of Date

15

The shad and asparagus are over, the berries
And late bluefish still to come: and yet beyond these wait
The successive New Years at harvest, mid-darkness and
Arisen spring—three points each of which could be a pure
Spot of origin, or a clear moment of closure.
As it is, they whirl by as bits of what is being
Measured rather than as milestones, as parentheses
Which turn out to have been what was being put between
Brackets in the first place. Occasions usurp the false
Fronts of giddy centers on circumferences. How
The lazy susan of the seasons turns around! piled
Chock-a-block with delectables, eased about by Time,
Our most thoughtful and, ultimately, murderous host.

Beginnings

16

I stood under a plain tree discoursing with someone
Lovely and young, or lay out upon the fancy lawn
Remembering a faraway body, recalling
A lost and distant laugh, recollecting disparate
Instants of delight in other seasons, other lands.
I stared down the halted water under willows that
Lay shadowed upon the dark shallows, and held my oar
Like a breath, the faraway wail of vanishing cars
Hanging in the active, evening air, my heart empty
Of souvenirs, my mind unwinding its arguments.
All these are within your nearby memory: remind
Me now of some moments mirrored in oblivion
As we stand silent beside some silent summer stream.

Amenable Locations

22

17

What there is to hear from the particular sea-mews
Homing in on our local point cuts through clarities
Of fair evening and the difficult radiance
Fog exhibits, high-noted observations whose tone—
High, personably middle or far from simply low—
Is muted by the sheer pitch of the wingèd outcry.
What there is to see in the running out and back in
Of our local inlet sighs, through barriers of firs
Along the low intervening islands, with rumors of
The ocean's legerdemain, which by mere sleight of land
Keeps taking back what ground it appeared to have given.
What there is to know from the touch of the silent wind's
Hand gathers these raw reports and sifts them for the truth.

Clarities of the Coast

18

The low wind, the loud gulls and the bare, egregious cry
Of a goat somewhere around the point the land urges
On the unteachable bay: these have taken of late
To commenting on our two forms—differently placed,
Each observable only in quite another kind
Of light—posed silently, sombre-hearted among them.
What they say is as unfathomable as what we
See, gazing out between mildly distant islands at
A horizon contrived by gray sky and gray water.
The nearby green water, with no memory of all
That distant amplitude of sea, slaps playfully at
These contemplative rocks which might be ourselves but for
Our darkening power to behold them and compare.

Further Clarities

The pine with but one thought regards the water against
Which it rises, the wide bay with so much on its mind—
Clumps of nearby island and smudges of distant rock,
Other firs at the end of the long meadow which cut
Into the water's extent of consciousness, and at
The faraway edge of the day, an elaborate
Serial narrative of sundown. Now a long yawl
Crawls wearily into sight: the pine of one idea
Points to it as if it should remind the water of
Something; but the bay, as if in some old joke about
Absorption, is reminded of the sky—everything
Reminding water of the sky—despite its bazaar
Of reflections. This puzzles the single-minded pine.

Opacities of the Pine

Firecrackers sounding like shots of handguns rattle
The afternoon of early July at a late time
For celebrations and it is an inglorious
Fourth we have come to, like the birthday of a very
Sick man: no simple affirmations will do today.
In the dying wind the nation's stars and stripes slacken;
I guess this must be the flag of its disposition
Not to save itself. Only now, much later, all flags
Down for the night, we watch some bunting—no more a flag
Than the flag is our old glory—as it fitfully
Gleams in the streetlamp's conditional light, like a truth
Which the sad, difficult telling of half-conceals, half-
Discloses, through our few tears ungleaming in the dark.

A Late Fourth

                    21   Oh,
━━━━━━━━━━   say can you see
                                 how our old
                                ten and two and
                                      one
Our thirteen starters twinkling, an original star
Flared up, a July fourth supernova, (memory
Watching starry rockets now in grandstands, or along
Chilly beaches) Can you see how then it exploded
Westward, southward, urging the hegemony of light
On hills of high, darkened cloud, unwilling plains, milky
Rivers and one-candled mountain-cabins of the night?
Democracy which closes the past against us (said
Tocqueville) opens the future up: but as you sit here
With me on the high rocks at Cape Eleutheria,
Truthful in your shawl, all the light that ever was shines
In your eyes, later to burn off tomorrow's blankness.

        22   *Sparklers*
━━━━━━━━━━

I have burned batches of cookies, formed rich tortes all wrong
From the start, propounded all-too-consistent puddings,
Lost hot cross buns, fussed unduly over cupcakes, turned
Bread—in one of those mundane, negative miracles—
Into stones, caused popovers to burst with windiness,
Launched Zechariah's flying rolls, filled Ezekiel's
Edible one (lamentation and mourning and woe
In equal parts, rising eloquently in long pans).
Now I am at the work of confection even when
Loafing, not irrelevantly, near the oven door
Where what goes on is no longer in my hands. All these
Maker's dozens come out right: I read your recipes
Now, remember your arm firm around the mixing bowl.

                                        Baker's Lament

23

To say that the show of truth goes on in our outdoor
Theatre-in-the-round may be no more than to remark
That one is always led out of some cave or other
Into the irritating glare of what is never
More than a high, wide, sunny, open local chamber
Of our general system of caves. But that it plays,
Night after night, under lights, drawing crowds even when
It is most archly stylized, let alone when lines are
Mouthed, and crotches scratched, in flatly stylized masquerades,
Means more. Truth sank all she had into this spectacle;
What's behind the scenes is openly part of the show,
As is everything that you lean over and whisper
To me knowingly as we watch one of the tryouts.

Long Run

24

When to say something of what stretches out there toward me
—Greens, rock grays, colors of water making up spaces
That speak to what we dream up as distance and depth—seems
Uncalled for, one is almost made to reproach oneself,
Asking, *How can one sing a strange song in the Lord's land?*
Mouth evasive and emphatic scat-lyrics of all
The mess of exile, there at the heart of a place famed
As the terminus of the longest expedition?
And yet, what had made one abandon each land was the
Blaring of some general canto, whose unisons
Comprised their own imperious mode of noisiness.
One rejoiced in an inward air as one underwent
Wandering: here still one must intone that undersong.

By the Waters

25

The universal great space, stately but ungrounded
Never seems, on star-guarded nights of enormous width,
To be our proper room, wherein we are, but rather
Where we are ever on the brink of being immersed
In what is beyond us and our being in the know.
And yet, on clouded midnights, all that outer black goes
Utterly blank, all the grains of light dissolving in
A mist of the implicit and the occluded; we
Are welcomed into what is a dim, high-ceilinged hall
We might as well be lords of. Impossibilities
Of too much openness having now clearly closed down,
The waters above muddied as if somehow for our
Own good, space retreats and makes way for us, and for room.

Our Place

26

I try to go new places with you, and yet we keep
Returning to so many of the old ones, sometimes
By lazy design, most often inevitably,
Given the unmapped ways that we take. This afternoon,
For instance, far up the beach people were gathered round
What would have had to be the event of the season:
A clam playing a harmonica or something like
That; and our walk along the wet sand where foamy hands
Kept rewriting their marginalia was halted
Short of that novelty. We were left with the renewed
Singularity of sundown behind the sand dunes,
The commentary that an eastern sea out of which
The sun rises keeps making upon the book of hope.

New Wrinkles

27

Words we have exchanged keep playing out their low treasons
Against the journals of the usual, the nocturnes
Of the odd, falling into line once they are uttered.
The parts of our discourse, which stretches out of sight far
Ahead and long behind, wait with the patience of those
Who have been truly used. Or far less complacently,
Twenty-eight thousand, five hundred sixty syllables
Here breathe hotly down the neck of some ultimate one
That may not demean their manyness. Means to some end,
They have been awaiting death. Endings mean meaning's end.
So the final monosyllable, with a volume
Thunderous and inaudible brings us to a close.
In the end as in the beginning will be the word.

At the End of the Line

28

I went out without you yesterday for a slow hour.
The lichens which in the right light give a choral tongue
To the rising rock were simply plastered over it;
The fir-woods began just at its circle of shadow;
The sun leaked down to the floor in interesting ways;
Here was here and there was there; all sorts of life astir
In among other, larger things were there merely for
The noticing—and yet noticing was not itself
A kind of drawing of breath, murmuring of pulse,
Let alone the mind's caress which shapes and loves at once.
Everything was clear and one thing: nothing came between
Me and where I was, there, amid a manageable
Jumble of evidence. This was this. And that was that.

The Fact of the Matter

What she and I had between us once, America
And its hope had; and just as I grieve alternately
For what I know myself to have lost of what had been,
And for all that loss I was suffering all that while
I was doing, I thought, so well, so goes the nation,
Grieving for her hope, either lost, or from the very
Start, a lost cause. All our states and I are one in this.
O my America, my long-lost land lady of
The hardening ground, the house neither ancient nor in
Good repair, the brackish stream, the half-abandoned mill,
The red plastic bucket that hung in the place we kept
By the beach where, I remember, August evenings
Rang with hilarity until we trembled with cold.

An Old Song

With you away on whatever other business you
May have, or going for a swim (the day being hot)
In perhaps some forest pool, all I can do, I find,
Is question or provoke. I wonder among the deep
Shades of my dusty study with its single candle
While my wandering eye surveys, in wild fields beyond,
The rusting iron in the ripening corn; I hear
What the July hot air noises emptily about.
Without you around to take seriously, I ask
"Well?" of the wind; "What?" of my dim working-place; "Wherefor?"
Of the rustic emblems of latter America.
The sad, ungainly cows of our land look up and mourn,
"Who needs a gadfly on the way to the slaughterhouse?"

Summer Questions

We are all at sixes and sevens not just about
The state of the nation but our state of contention
Itself, you maintaining that repose is a snaffle
In exuberance's mouth, I that quarreling is
A cave where the spirit sits deafened and dumbfounded.
You rise to the bait of what I refuse to stand for.

Arguments of heat cool off in bed where arguments
Of light are dimmed in horizontal ways of being
At odds. Rough, pleasurable strife resolves nothing but
Minimizes differences for the while we lie
Silent together in apposition that is true
Friendship. —*No*, you say, as if to awaken sleeping
Amity to its daily work of debate once more.

Nay, calls strife's reveille. I disagree; and we're at
A new kinds of odds, in which my braying out of *Yea*
Shivers the morning air into little blasts of wind.
But this smacks far less than ever of domestic farce—
No fear lest dinner burn, say, while unheated, genial
Discourse propounds itself in the next room; no fear lest
Argument drop idly to the floor like a dishrag
The while Judy throws what was to have been lunch at Punch.

Your side of the story? Starting out with unhoarse nay—
Saying? Well, without me, you would never have it told:
Your tacit dissents are heard only in inference
From my affirmatives, yeas echoing unheard nays.
I'll give you eight to five that at bottom we agree.

Disagreements

After one of our unheated arguments, I heard
Two shepherds (well, not shepherds really, but let us say
They were) contending, beneath a verdant shade about
To give in to autumn, over their contention. A:
All of what we say in the first cool of early fall
Can only be a palinode to parting summer,
A recantation of easy heat. Sez you, says B,
What we sing is a prelude to the sober beauties
And late passions of the ember months. Says A, *To be*
Truthful for the moment——interrupted B: *For Aye* . . .
But both agreed on you: how in your very breathing
Their debate resolved, in the A, B of your heartbeat.
(I can assure you of this, who made these shepherds up.)

Eclogue

Wholly concerned for the mass of the pieces that we
Carve day by day, we feel none the less put upon when
The consequences of their profiles are finally
Laid at our door. But how not to have what we had meant
Remain forever on the under-surfaces? How
To keep what it had been all about from lighting out
Suddenly, the night before completion, with what cash
And negotiable securities there were? Keeping
The finished piece in darkness is out of the question;
Yet not minding that it will be got wrong is harder
Than carving itself, than the work of roughing-out fine
Attention which, not like an abused servant giving
Notice, rather trembles on the verge of taking it.

I thought that you might have something to recommend in
Re this plague of misunderstandings which come buzzing
In when we run up the flag—on some holiday, or
Perhaps to show the children how it is properly
Done—and hang around in a brown, noisy cloud until
Hours after sunset. You have seen such visitations
Come and go, and I picture you smiling placidly
Through the most alarming crowding of the summer nights
With the stings and wails of nasty, pick-up orchestras,
Or, attended by the two young Misses Construction
And Apprehension, presiding over an ornate
Interior. Proof, yourself, against being got wrong,
You I hope can show me how to cope with all of this.

Being Got Wrong

Well, now, the year having finally come to a head
Here at the end of summer, you and I can begin
Again in the crispness of things: the new honeyed taste
Of a bright, hard apple of the early fall, the look
Of the next chapter in the annals of yearning as
Reflected in the quickening of its bright first page.
But the brightest leaf turns over, its shadowed face down
On the dark ground. We thrust into the middle of things
Even at their start, surprised by the forenoon's fine snap,
By the skip half-hidden in each of our steps, thankful
To have been preserved and sustained by the very wind
That blows away the summer, to have reached this season.
We will have to look into the matter of winter.

Very well, then, what now? There are resolutions far
Easier kept than made, acts of connection between
The speaker and the spoken-to (and -for) easier
Done than said: you know this well, whose speaking is my deed,
As I, remembering a quiet listener of
My youth, whom my inept, yearning touch penetrated
In a smooth moment and darkly dazzling, for which
There were no words and never would be. For the new year
I shall not promise you anything more, then, than what
Is strongly done even if lamely said: "I'll try";
"I will be tried"—hard threats hidden in soft predictions.
You, who promise nothing, thus ever give, as you have,
With your eyes, the gentle smiling of impure surprise.

Starting Up in the Fall

38

Where has it gone, that long recent summer when the mind
Sported with waves along an ever-brightening beach?
There was a long look to be taken both up and down
The miles of strand toward where dune and sky vanished in light.
Wisdom had come from the wizening of Christendom,
It seemed; gleaming chariots would leap forth on the land
At the sound of the breaking of all the cruel old chains.
Around the bonfires at evening, ceremonials
Sent up sparks into the black air: the drawing aside
Of the curtains of flesh revealed what in the firelight
Appeared to be the figure of joy, yet bondage lurked
Invisibly in the shadows of the emptiness.
Summer gone, what work is it we must get back to now?

Cool Days

39

The fall wind, a maddened Santayana, rips the leaves
Out of the volume of our lives when the day's reading
In the chilled park is over; a sibyl of rubble,
Who flings them no great distance to where the garbled heap
Of verbiage goes on with its old unsightliness;
A discounted cantor who intones the text about
Which we shall always be outraged and against which our
Bookish bodies yet cry out like leaves composting in
Their hay for our now unrestricted clay, when the last
Worms shall have their treat and dust shall be the serpent's meat;
But at the last, a word-swallower at the great, red
Autumnal fair, who silences our last dying moan
And snuffs out the final rhymes of breathing with his own.

Destroyer

We ramble along up-hill through the woods, following
No path but knowing our direction generally,
And letting fall what may we come up against the worn
Fact that all this green is second growth—reaches of wall
Knee-high keep appearing among low moments of leaf;
Clearings, lit aslant, are strewn across old foundations.
This is of course New England now and even the brook,
Whose amplified whisper off on the right is as firm
A guide as any assured blue line on a roadmap,
Can never run clear of certain stones, those older forms
Of ascription of meaning to its murmuring, as
We hear it hum *O, I may come and I may go, but . . .*
Half-ruined in the white noise of its splashing water.

One of Our Walks

If I were a different person with a different sort
Of occupation, I might show you, on some late walk
Through a part of the city you had not seen before,
My place of business; you might even meet a few of
The workers there, their presences graced by anecdote
Perhaps, and then we might stand out on the pier looking
Over the harbor and its lights. But I own no mills
Of dark red brick; so walk no further than where we are
Now: meet my unembodied helpers—Jenny, spinning
Out the thread of discourse; Dolly, trundling along her
Bulky objects; Jack lifting and Doc Crane unloading;
Poor lazy John who cleans out the gleaming bowl; and bright
Molly, bolting the tall gilded mirror to the wall.

Where I Work

Now I walk with you through the ruins of the city
Of Glyph, low piles of rubble on a low hill under
A baking sun, shuddering at how close to nothing
A wise king's walls and postern gates became. Like all true
Ruminators over wreckage we console ourselves
That words may still strike live sparks from even this dead rock,
That enchanted documents outlast the monuments,
Marmoreal dust survived by the memorial
Light of the word. So with me conversing you forget
All time, and amid the ruins of ancient chaos
I stand with—and I want to say, "thee"—making a fresh
Start, in an oasis of our saying, knowing that
We will be outlived by what of green we have given.

Ah, but the lions of time sharpen their claws against
These rocks of book, wearing away powerful reasons
And sovereign rhyme; and the old tale they told themselves
—The moony-eyed idolaters of broken columns—
Was that their scrawls would endure, even as the endeared
Squares of the sidewalk where they played marbles in the spring
Outgloried Rome etcetera. And if the whole tale
Does not exactly crumble into mindless dust, still
All words lose their sizzling edges in time, blunted
By inexactitude, our race being unable
Now to heft any weight of meaning. So with our words:
Your heart hardens; my will softens to wool; your sight sighs,
And my wide mind narrows its grasp to what is merely mine.

Some Walks with You

This whole business of outliving—it is as if, once,
One mild summer evening we were sitting outside,
Eating a few leftovers, when two great Presences
Came by, tired, and in their gentle way quite ravenous,
And we shared all of what little we had with them, and
Not that the bottle and the few bowls refilled themselves,
But that you and I were emptied of our appetites
That mild summer evening under the slumbering
Green of low trees, and that the departing Presences
Left us with the gift of a common moment of death.
An old story. Yet for all practical purposes,
When I go, you go—whether or not a laurel bush
And a myrtle just then spring up there outside our house.

But for all impractical purposes, you'll outlast
Me, who'll endure not in memory, merely in soft
Clay. You were around before we met (I, too, but with
That fascinating difference we keep trying to
Figure out): whatever you taught me was for your own
Survival, even though I've subsisted on it too.
Talking you up as I do among unlistening
Branches and heedless gardens, beside uncaring parked
Cars along a noisy street, may just be playing down
Your words, as if the script of summer midnight you were
Starring in were one you couldn't ever have written.
What will it be, then: a condition of evergreen?
A state of starlight? We'll consider it for a while.

Talking You Up

How charming—magical, fragile both, I mean—the time
When Past was like a dungeon, Present a wide forecourt
Looking further out at open, sunny future fields;
Or when some hidden room in the dark house of childhood
Had to be ransacked to profit what one hoped to be.
Not so now: the Hall of Records is all skylight glass,
And the starlight of the coming centuries which winks
And beckons will have been coming from aeons before.
Yet, loosed from the dark past, looking out through the picture
Window of California at a mile-wide future
Unformed save at the hands of the moment's comfiness,
X sips the honey of unproblematic sundown
And takes a long drink of the milk of amnesia.
Y, back east, asks what came before us, and what lies there.

Letting in Light

The figure ahead of us on the trail, looking back
From an easy stance of pause belying the extreme
Difficulty of the country: he has gone before
Both in that it was in the past that he trod the ground
Which now we stand on looking at him with far less ease
Than he, and that he waits before our gaze like a part
Of the high trail itself. His glance, open but clearly
Asymmetric, borrows flashes of sunlight among
Leaves of underbrush to do its winking with, winking
Of acknowledgment that he knows what we know of him,
Preposterous graybeard with a touch of the farouche,
Behind us and ahead of us at once, one eyebrow
High overarched there in his momentary bower.

Still, the trail lies all before us. Neither alone, nor
With a tour, you and I walk our own kind of *via*
Media. Even when he or she accompanies
My rambles of the afternoon, you will be walking
At my other hand, pointing out how immediate
Presences—the gray, unquestionable rock I see,
The untranslatable, loud wind I hear—yield themselves
To the scentedness, warm of blood, full of heart, of the
Living thing midway between them. Moving up the path
With you is as if mounting some trim companionway
From the ingenious turbines up to the high points
Of lookout, not rejecting where we had been before
But bearing a part of what was into what will be.

On the Trail

49

An anecdote: I sat here in this chair last month, and—
Wow! you came up right behind me, startling me so that
I broke the last word off the line I had been working
At, abandoning the feature-story of despair
I had been fashioning, and turned back to see whether
You had deliberately crept up to rob me of
The last word, or whether simply to tell me someone
From Porlock or from Washington had telephoned me.
What ever could you have thought to do with that missing
Word? Pelt me with it, as with a berry in a broad
Field of fruited bushes we were slowly moving through?
Feed it to me, in the starlight, in some ultimate
Rebuke? I'll never know, but you've helped me mend my ways.

The Last Word

50

Your games of hiding: the one you played this afternoon
In the Memorial Park, where you walked by the lake
(The shadow upon it of the old bow bridge was more
Of a way of getting across reflective water
Than the cast-iron arch itself): one moment, and you
Were gone. Then I heard laughing from the rocks that I used
To play on as a child, mica winking in the sun,
And saw you standing half-hidden in a niche, shadows
Of frivolous leaves falling across your summer dress.
Your other game of hiding in the dark . . . In return
I play my games and bury an old coin in your cake,
Or put an artificial pressed flower between two
Leaves of my intimate journal where I know you'll look.

And Go Seek

Now: There was a tall girl once whom I mistook for you
—Or was it you I thought was she? (Just like a tall tale
From some lovely book that I had not allowed myself
To see the figurative meaning of at all). My
Heart was dim, the lady's name was light; how gently once
We sang, I now remember, in Indiana in
The summer night, and she warmed my distant winter that
December. Unchained to the letter now, your spirit
Plays hide-and-seek, now in the fair and tall, now in the
Dark and small. I am most near it sometimes when hiding
My impatient eyes, counting to fourteen, piercing your
Disguise. Here I Come, Ready Or Not. Where are you, Love?
The tall girl's long gone, it is a summer night again.

August Recall

All the singing rivers commend our rivery songs:
The estuary at New London hummed an old theme
Softly in the revised standard version of the Thames;
The harsh Jordan, narrow enough in the Middle-East
In the middle-west snaked through the campus, a toy stream;
The slow Charles led me to its source in the trickling Cam.
The East River wedded to the river that is west;
The conjunctive Harlem, where to spite the devil once
I spun in a folding kayak with an older guide;
The dirty Cuyahoga; the tall Connecticut;
Tiber and Danube, Rhine and Seine of which enough said—
Who will chant the silence that celebrates their orgy
Of confluence when at last they join the Stygian flood?

Principal Rivers

53

Patterns of light and flakes of dark breaking all across
The surface of the stream—rhyming words of wave, strophes
Of undulation, echoings of what just had been
Going on upstream a ways—we like to take all these
As matters of surface only, as part of the shaping
Or framing of the banks. But that would make the water
Stagnant and silent, whose face gives no interesting
Access to its depth. Yet when the brook gets to babbling,
Really has something to say for itself, the surface
—Broken, flashing, loud—changes place with what depths there are.
Then what forms on top will have been troped up from below,
And the otherwise soundless and motiveless bottom
Will be constantly noisy with the figures of light.

Reading the Brook

54

Mademoiselle de la Moon gazes at her gleaming
In the ever-hungering sea's midnight waves. "My Queen,"
Sir Water seems to sing, "I am subject to your light,
Your will betides well or ill for my very motions."
Yet the wailing main need not crave favors: he has made
The cold moon up, projected her out of his flashings
And phosphorescences onto the fire-bearing night,
Rolled his wet lamplight into a round mirroring rock.
His rough surface shapes an object to be subject to.
There are too many reflections on mirrors by far
As it is for me to dwell upon the parable,
And for once the firstness of the sun does not apply:
This is a matter only of moon and ocean-light.

Reflections of Desire

55

That great, domed chamber, celebrated for its full choir
Of echoes: high among its shadowed vaults they cower
Until called out. What do echoes do when they reply?
Lie, lie, lie about what we cried out, about their own
Helplessness in the face of silence. What do they do
To the clear call that they make reverberate? *Berate,*
Berate it for its faults, its frangible syllables.
But in this dear cave we have discovered on our walks
Even a broken call resounds in all, and wild tales
We tell into the darkness return trimmed into truth.
Our talk goes untaunted: these are the haunts of our hearts,
Where I cry out your name. Hearing and overhearing
My own voice, startled, appalled, instructed, I rejoice.

Under the Dome

56

We need not visit this big metal archway in which
The not-too-distant other shore is framed. In the west,
A famous bold parabola propounds its puzzle.
Here, far from that high paradigm of openness, looms
Our local hyperbola, more thick and squat, merely
Huge. The writers come to gawk at its blandly smoother
Curvature, to misconstrue its inner space, which is
Only an emptiness, not a leaping-up of room.
Admiring its high gleam, they do not see the mocking
Dark lower branch of their hyperbolic arch extend
Itself downward, dropping through the complementary
Air above some park at the other end of the earth,
The statuary of admiration doubly botched.

Travel Note

The Queen of the Parade floats by on her painted car,
Glitteringly, in between postures—sitting for some
Endless series of portraits? lying for the moment?
Standing for the brave Muse of Parading who could not
Make it this afternoon? Ten streets ahead The Old Men's
Band plays *A Closer Walk with Thee* as chromatic tints
Of something bouncy in another key fall across
Its dying sounds. Held down by long guy-ropes in the hands
Of struggling lackeys, the Great Forms float by overhead—
Pegasus, Apollo, a Hippogriff, Daffy Duck:
In childhood, knowing that these balloons were full of air
Deflated in no way whatever stature they had.
Now we gaze sadly, bored, at the Triumph of Moments.

But the Queen will not be forsworn. She turns her head, smiles,
And waves at us amid even more oompahs, sirens
Cutting the distant air, seducing all attention
To the violent island all around us, away
From this tacky-tawdry ill-timed progress, this parade
Of tired fables which is now an institution.
But the sirens are tired too and have all belonged
For some years to the Society of Sound Effects.
They are as part of a neighboring parade the Queen
Will also loll amidst, begrimed as beglittered now.
Her smiles go on for miles; the great balloons will preside
Over the darkening streets, over the lackeying
Layers of lower air they gravely bow and sway among.

Pageant of the Cold

59

The Fun-House of the fairgrounds once stood here. Inside were
Contrivances so tacky that, far from scorning them,
Now, we value them as antiquarian machines.
No restoration could bring back the effects—the room
Of multiplications; the mazes inside mazes;
Reversing chambers where we were condemned to getting
On with things ass-backwards. Jokes—about penetrations,
About the One and the Many, about buggery,
Were born there, buried now in graffiti (*One can buy*
Balm for any disappointment:/I'll board you forward
Without need of ointment—as if that could end something!)
When the doors slid shut behind one and there was dark, that
Was origination; when they opened into bright
Sunlight, that was closure. One was out of there for good.

Public Landmarks I

60

The old Melpomene Theatre right across the street
From the Gaiety, itself a singer of sad songs,
Was in its time a revival house and now awaits
A new developer, someone who will see that when
Its old façade is broadened slightly, its back wall brought up
A bit, the shortening of the room will yield no less
Depth, and more flexibility for the inner space:
Ad hoc arrangements, temporary rooms, openings
And closures, so that one will be more free in less space.
This house of ex-*aiaiai*, scene of the formerly
Tragic, this theatre of recapitulations
Then will shed new light in an old place, whatever may
Be playing there, ancient words watching from the shadows.

Public Landmarks II

It was not for such fragments that we wandered so far
A field, a mountain, an old city by a river.
But more and more the broken pieces we saw in our
Meanderings came to have a power to command
Devotion that the unfractured images themselves
—Venus entire, a solemn family on a grave
Stele—could never have had at their time, let alone
From us. So we see these interruptions of an arm's
Extent, these abstract structures replacing familiar
Dispositions of the body's tribe of parts, these shapes
Of breakage passing over faces like traces of
Thought, and knowing how they figure our way of being
In our bodies, we believe in them as in ourselves.

We consider this archaic maiden who has lost
Her head over time, and gained her patch of fractured stone
Here, along a newly conceived plane, more personal
Than the half-ineffability of her fixed grin.
Stone can hardly be in pain, yet this has undergone
Something beyond its original shaping, something
Beyond that origin of feeling an inner edge
Of the outside world, the end of oneself. But in the
Light of our dry brooding, figure yields its truth to form;
Form returns to marble; and to broken stone we cry
"Good! You deserved it! What flesh has always had to know
You now have learned." Yes, but when stone has been turned into
A trope, what we see fractured here will be heartbreaking.

Breakage

46

63

Here by the ruins of this fountain where water played
With stone while the light was playing with it, long sessions
Were held on pleasant afternoons, with talk of shadows
Seated on the sunny grass, of substance there along
The marble benches. There they walked together with their friends
Laurie, Stella, Delia, Celia, Bea and the others.
But over on the hill there were those who spoiled the fun—
Dirty old Dick Dongworth, his mighty line no longer
Standing for him (when their stichs go limp even Uncle
Walt's dildo won't do for them any more), and Louise
Labia, her heart an open book—eye your body
From their past, as we pass by the places where they lurked
Jealous of the others, too early to have met you.

Dreams and Jokes

64

Now that you bid me write of what she and she-sub-one
And she-sub-n and I did at those various times
Of darkness in the working day and the knowing night,
My truant pen writes with French letters: *je, ma muse, et . . .*
Your laughter hides in the spaces of my stammering.
We may be our own blank sheets, but ink can never come
Clean about the heart of matters like those you remind
Me of, our oldest sports played on the fields of ourselves,
Our briskly-danced adagios that now enact the old
Moments from behind their zigzag comitragic masks.
But what are the words in amor's low language for deeds?
All said and done, Love's wordless sword is mighty as the
Pen is, which mars our sad amusing talk of Venus.

Your Command

65

Heroic Love danced on our stage awhile, in the dark
Of the days that shone and shook with Heroic Battle.
But that act was over by the time Sir John Failstiff mocked
Love: "Sock it to me—that's what half-mooning's all about,"
He chortled, brandishing a dirty sock. Even then
The slack-jawed face appealed to the bumpkin in the hay
Or in the back seat of the car, its wordless message
Flashed out "Have me, I'm hopeless" or blinked its "Now now now."
Now the dance is Love for All, love well lost for the world,
The risks taken are those of intimacy; love fell
A casualty of the unceremonial,
Laughed at by the wind in our heckling, red leaves, themselves
Gone the way of the whirled, fallen to mere easiness.

The Lovers

66

In the old anecdotes of amor they still allude
To in brittleness of feeling, the master of arch
Ceremonies, the perpetrator of injustice,
Takes after his father Mars who, they keep forgetting,
Is always in the picture; and thus they can complain—
Speaking of earlier enactments of their cases—
"On love's disputed ground, on bed of war, they both lay,
Fallen soldier, fallen whore—how unfair, this falling!"
As for falling in love: O, if one were said to rise
In it then—all being foul in these matters—so should
One have to rise in battle, or asleep, as if one
Thereby were moving away from—rather than toward—the,
After all, irrelevant fall of our finale.

The Fall

48

67

The crime of Onan probably was not that lonely
Joy, but sullenly refusing to get on with his
Brother's business, choosing to cop out suddenly, there
On the spot. This was the lonely sorrow he begot:
Abandoning the work for dream or musing, not love
Of hand (in neither case abusing self, or delight
Or some poor Other's lot.) But if just now, I withdraw
From some well-loved form that lies here, half-done, half-composed
On the lined sheet where we have come together, it is
Hardly to shun the work of making, but to get on
With it, turning, in the darkness of our lamplit tasks,
To your new phantom, lying by the old one you fled,
But with me ever, body in body, hand in hand.

The Abandoned Task

68

All our cheap, failed love-stories are old tales told even
In the dear language of Paradise: Poor Al F. finds
That one hot, urgent night on the front porch comes to mean
Not just having Beth, but ever after having her
On his hands (she is no mere doll it turns out). A roll
In the unmown hay keeps unrolling an alphabet
Of episodes, the tête-à-tête descends to fumbling,
Then the consequences of the cough of fulfillment.
Lamed Memsahib of noon, she limps through the tawdry bush
Of daily life. Who is to pay? The frail-bosomed fay
Lady of the car back-seat and queen of the front porch?
The fancy dancer who barked his shin on the next day?
Their sin was surviving their desire. The end was tough.

Literal Account

Like some ill-fated butterfly, the literalists
Try to pin down—its illustrious wings extended
Not in eloquence, but unwittingly—the fragile
Spirit of doting, at all those layers of remove
From brass tacks. Yet after all, brass tacks get lost in time,
While what one was asked to get down to them from endures.
Thus: young, before sweets of doting had soured into doubt,
I made an idol of the image of her figure,
Until one soft night I found it squirming there beneath
My grateful but unbelieving body, in a bed
Borrowed but smooth with moonlight—at which the idol was
Destroyed, its shaping of desire usurped by the skill
Of remembrance, in her realm of frail-winged images.

Lepidoptery

Like prisoners released from cells built by their touching
Itself, hot walls firming up every hot new minute,
Bars worming gently into place with no more clanging
Than the close sound of breath, one after another they,
The lovers, emerge into the quiet after-court.
The sobbing of their bodies . . . for loss of what had gripped
Them, as for joy at being outside themselves once more
Their soft jails, spun out of their hearts . . . I would not have said
"Cocoons," but you pointed to the window-glass, battered
By gypsy moths, imprisoned without, souls in ancient
Mysteries, alighted on the corners of windy
Pyramids, fed on the wisdom from lacy pages
Of the now-tattered hieratic book of the woods.

Soul and Body

"Pleasures and pains, pleasures and pains, when a man's married
His songs are refrains, his texts well-worn misquotations,
His passionate homilies unwittingly cribbed from
The standard handbooks of harangue."—This itself, quoted
From some other well-meaning manual, is as one
With the "passionate homilies" it would interpret
In just the way the homilies did not want to be
Taken. What can we learn about Wisdom, then, from all
The Handbooks of Handbooks? What avails the way in which
Cool, old voices of distance are heard screaming? in which
Homely points of needles and pins bright and dulled, grander
Views of homeliness, and yet loftier points from which
Grandeur is put in its place, stand on the same cold ground?

The Foundation

Oh, yes, the animals were a hard act to follow:
Through all the stages of creation, the vaudeville
Of coupling unfolded until without much of an
Intermission the first of us were sent out, partners
Evolving their routine even on the night itself.
Thus that now old business of human-see, human-do.
Had we come on first, rather than late to our last act,
Had beasts learned from us to come together in benign,
Obedient turns, what of our nobler parts? What of
The wing-caped, glittering rider of the fierce horses
We are now below the waist?—High and low, anima
And animal, all one in us, bodies entering
One another would be our most figurative dance.

Animal Acts

73

The aftermath of epiphany was not just yet
Once more a round of delights and celebrations of
The vision of misrule; no delayed instant replay
Of the party; no mere lowering of last night's jests,
Sir Toby Fart now on a diet, Malfolio
Grousing in some incomprehensible dialect.
The Low was always there, wedded to the High before:
Rapt Viola fiddled with words, diddling them till they
Came; the copulars of syntax played sexual parts
Of speech in the oldest learned jokes. Our afternight,
A bit longer, sadder, even more contrariwise,
Has turned the banquet tables on the wearied games that
Put decorum, poor devil, in his own hell of fun.

High and Low

When, aping the literary lover, his eye filled
With one star, I at eighteen tried rhyming into bed
A tall, dark girl named Barbara, now dead, everyone
Had an earful of my earnest conceits, studious
Wit, and half-concealments of the way I'd hoped we'd end
Up; and the more contrived my rhyming became, the more
It meant about desire (this the ear-filled ones could not
Understand). I marvelled, dazed, at what was done by less
Textual souls for fun; I hoped to, like the girl-shy
Yeats, pass through the tenderest of gates, and discharge with
A mighty spasm in her deep, romantic chasm.
The truth was that, though she and I rhymed a few times, my
Young words on their paper sheet had far more joy than we.

And thus in writing "of" this one or that, sending open
Allusive letters to A or elusive letters
To the world in re B, I was arising from the
Dreaming cot of language onto the teeming streets where
A's and B's and ampersands awash with C's and D's
Filled the air with their din. We had not met, nor could I
Have heard your soft voice if we had. All this is just to
Say yesterday I found a second-or-third-hand
Copy of my earliest verses, Barbara and
Willow-willow and that ilk, inscribed—of course—with your
Name. After a while, some moving-day, you'd passed me on.
But it seems that some fair monitor even then made
Lust and wit hold hands, heard passion in the studied leaves.

Erotic Lyrics

When we were all fourteen, the sharper our visions were
—Say, of the body of the neighbor's girl at her bath
Framed in the half-opened window across the courtyard,
Say, of her memory of young Heathcliff on the black
And white screen that afternoon—the more distant from touch.
Staying in a sense fourteen, even as we were all
Getting older, kept something alive—the girl's image
Blurred as she lay beside us in the bed of springtime,
The actor's face coarsened into color and substance,
Yet the Sublime kept climbing its ladder as the flood
Waters rose from the cellars; something beyond contact
Kept touch constantly aspiring to it, even when
The mind wandered, even to being fourteen again.

The structures and agitations of the older ways
Of handling matters of love, then housed and empowered
Other spirits—it was as if an old tomb could be
Recast and made into a series of monuments
Of reconsideration, with the base as of old,
A new frieze, somewhere in which the antiquarians
Might discern an image of the old tomb as it was,
And a new roof open to the stars. But these places
Are empty now: neither lovers, nor thinkers in the
Light of the afternoon, lurk about them any more.
But they stood for so much more than they were built to bear,
And for so long, memorials to the masonry
Of the ideal, as if love hung ever aloft.

The age of sixteen, in its infinite wisdom, puts
Lightly aside mere fourteen's joys and terrors. And thus
With our larger histories: the temples all rebuilt,
Modern love went it all the better, hung two more strings
On the old, echoing instrument, strung two more lines
Across the alley-way to hang the dirty laundry
Out, for the truthful wind to comment on in detail
(Underpants flapping like the triumphant flags of love
Smocks blown into the clefted folds they had been worn to
Conceal). Now, when love and thought take their evening walks
They linger to talk along the widened peristyle
And slightly lowered elevation of a folly
Like this one in the public gardens we know so well.

Songs & Sonnets

79

Let's call it quits: I never long for you any more.
But the matter of your voice low in the late lamplight
My heart minded over for so long, the substance of
Your morning shadow dancing on the floor as you dressed,
The evening shadow of your body's depth, stand here
Demanding some ceremony now. Some fuss. Let's call
It quits. Addressing what I've just said, you reply then
Cheerily, "Hi, Quits!" We giggle and have done for now
With lying, not against half-truths so much, but telling
Tales against the other—falsehood—halves of whatever
We really mean by saying what we feel. "Hi, Quits!" "*Quits*"
(Like all his clan of feelings) grumbles, not at the joke,
But rather at having been given a name at all.

The Resolution

80

A book: as I read it the letters keep decaying
Into illegibility, as if they had been
Poorly xeroxed to begin with. I awake, seeing
Behind my lids the blank of erasure and hearing
Only the surrounding murmur of four walls, hummed in
By silence, and asking if this meant you would leave me.
Even as I write this dream down my pen consumes it,
As the page's famished surface uses up the pen.
That the pain of most private loss could not be published;
That without you I remain not nothing, but something
Blank; that the dream-book's roughened leaves turn to green again
Only because you allow your paintbrush to be used—
These darken into truth as in sympathetic ink.

The Dream of the Book

Once you and I—but no fables now. Tell what there was:
Once within a place she and I were together in
The way that fictions about our lives can be: each one
Feeling not for, but by means of the other, so that
Soft converse in the dying daylight penetrated
Both of us, who therewith felt each other's and our own
Deeps; and acts of darkness in the quickening night made
Discursive the room, the house, where all were imbedded.
But after, away here in the noise of circumstance
I scribble alone at the old story: *Once upon*
A time, she and I were together in the way that
Only those who have had the intelligence of love
And the experience of loss can etcetera.

"Yes, go on! This is plain talk of plainer feelings now,
Passion and pain in their imperative moods," cry the
Ninnies of experience. Fools of the omphalic
And the literal nod in comprehension. The soft
Coins stamped "STRONGLY FELT" clatter down the receptive slots
Of the automata of actuality, who
Start in on their dance of being deeply moved. When those
Unstrung puppets wind up their timely and mindless act,
All the ninnies buzz off to supper. Then you and I
Are finally alone, beyond the din of their ken.
Moonlight enters our unlit room and projects a bright
Shape on the wall outlined by our shadows, a figure
Of our connectedness, of what we have between us.

Twice-Told Tale

Meet me here in the middle of the woods where I am
Making a path out from the clearing that you showed me
Months ago (now so overgrown with a thick muchness,
Merely more of the same—nothing summing it all up).
Moments of maximum penetration leave one with
Minimal resources for escape, and the thread of
Memory is all I have to lead me out of this
Mess of amazing amusements I've been working through:
Mid-forest musics (Haydn in the woods?), overnight
Mushroomings of weird, pale incident. Come find me now
—Mind the turning ways!—and we'll make do: there's more than wild
Material enough to stretch. We are two, but there's
Making what you always lovingly call both ends meet.

Letter

The heart of the matter? It throbs laboriously
—X says—amid shovelfulls of exasperation,
Neatly sawn cords of tedium, and sorting out brads
From endless nails. Not so—says Z—it leaps trembling at
The first strains of the body's serenade, at the light
In the clear blue window hinting that the door below
Will soon be unlocked. But at the living core—asks Y—
Slightly off the center, does not the pointed, rounded
Emblem cut into the contemplative tree not lie?
What Y means in the matter of the heart pictured there
Is that such inscriptions to the long moments of pause
On our walks beat out a general pulse: you and I
Figured in cut letters, the point of it all, the source.

The precisely central point of anything must be
Another matter, though. Small wondering schoolboys will
Submit a compass-pinprick, or an *I*'s dot that might
Mark out a dead center, to a microscope and see
The point getting lost in a wide, vague range of middle
Ground. But in its most contracted state the center stands
(Everything lies around it, it is about nothing),
Center of origin, equidistance, silent rest
And pointlessness. For only in the meddling schoolboys'
Destructions of certainty do areas arise,
Dim, jagged of bound, unexplored, in which one might roam
Ever dangerously, yet safe in the dark knowledge
That mapping these places means covering everything.

In the dim, indeterminate part of these woods, where
What we broadly call the middle of the excursion
—A place of being most amidst, not at an exact
Point of center—one has been ascending all morning,
Pushing on with joyful effort. Here is no-man's-land,
Ever contested for by starting and finishing.
From here on, downhill all the way: children run and laugh,
The older ones begin to creep, struggling now against
Descending itself, more than in the worst up-hill climb.
It is worse to have gravity pulling one onward
Than tugging one back from behind, restraining mere wild
Leaps upward. After the middle that grim force drags us
Not back to a starting-point, but on to the last place.

The Midst of It

These two tales I tell of myself and the life I led
To its destruction, one dark, one bright: one gathered from
A few gleaming moments—a slice or two of the cake
From where it was perfectly marbled—the other one
Rising from an undersong of despair. In neither
Case is the truth of the story—or the story of
The possibility that either one could be true
Or false at all—of any interest. What matters
Is what they might be good for: the story of a lost
Joy, as a sad anchor to drop below the surface
Of where we keep on going; the other version of
What was, the tale of a hell escaped, easily sounds
Like a noisy breath of wind filling my patched old sails.

Tales of the Sea

88

I'd not thought that drowning would be so like an easy
Ascent of some low but quite important hill: the tank
Into which I was descending of my own accord,
Lined with the light of some pale blank green, I was surprised
But not disturbed to find was set with convenient
Hand-holds for speeding one's progress downward with. But then,
As if you had recalled me in my own voice somehow,
Or as if some deeper shadow in the tank had stayed
My sinking, I turned quickly from shallow sleep, sank back
Into the self whose image I was when in the tank.
Telling you this now, I learn that the drowning-dream meant
Nothing, but would merely (had I not let go the hand-
Holds and turned up toward my bed again) have been my death.

The Dream of the Deep

The lion is the king of the beasts. We are the ace,
Contemplating his tawniness, color of dusty
Sunlight fallen on stone worn smooth; contemplating yet
The crown that his very image in itself upholds;
And, finding in his eminence the type of our own,
Seeing it was our high eye for hierarchy that
Enthroned him. Even now we know that others exceed
His power—the cow who shod and fed the white hunter,
Mannlicher in his bearing, the trypanosome in
His blood that brings the lion down—these are fierce satraps,
Victims themselves nonetheless, of the lordship of man
And of inhuman disaster. Two careless jacks thus
Dispense the bidding of the one-eyed great lord of life.

But now we are talking of what lies beyond the range
Of the visible, away from the gaze of the old
Hand-held cameras, beyond the ken of old John Reel,
Gnarled, reasoned white hunter of desire, huddled over
The spoor of the moment, which can lead him only on
Into the uninterestingness of the high grass.
The king of being hides in the labyrinth of size,
Not of mere turns of the way: we must move inside the
Very traces of traces themselves—there must we go,
Within, within, to find his double-spiralled cord spun,
Once thought, by the fates, a gossamer thread that leashes
The lion and binds our destinies, poor jokers, who
Still take our few tricks with the lion's magnificence.

Our Dominion

Cutting pages in a book—upward, across, again
Upward—I hear the various leaves sigh in their own
Several tongues: *"Enfin!"* whispers the slim, gray volume
Evenings in Marrakech (I translate); *"Endlich!"*—this
From the serious, sick treatise on "Unendingness"
(As close as English can come to that); and a long gasp,
"At last!" from the great folio of my earlier years.
Facing pages must at least once in their lives get to
Look out even at a pair of idly focussed eyes,
Let alone up past them to some kind of ceiling; light
Must be let in between them, lest the blind marriage of
Page one forty-four to one forty-five imprison
Them in their locked, unembracing gaze, their bundled sleep.

Chopping down a tree with names carved in its bark, mine and
Hers—not unwittingly, like some frenzied or condemned
Hero of high romance initiating our brute,
Obstinate compulsion to outlast our good names for
A while, but like a homesteader of the great heartland
Clearing a space for what will come to be—I took less
Of an ax to the past than the present already
Had, and heard no desiccated Dryad cry out *"Ouch!"*
Or *"Remember me!"*—the tree was no poetical
Oak, but softwood, waiting to be pulped, rolled, dried and bleached.
And it is you I now stand eye to eye with above
This ruled page that mirrors each to the other, while yet
Hiding my face from my own gaze, yours even from yours.

Opening Up

"Every soul is unique, and, thereby, original:
It is only when it employs the body to make
Something of something else, or utter something, that it
Falls into the nature of being imitative."
—So Doctor Reinkopf, overseer of the leaky jars
Of our lives. If he is right, the uncracked pots we shape,
Our noble tombs and numberless innovations, all
Come out of old Being-in-the-Body's pattern-book.
What of our walking, then? One would not want to remark
"What an original way of walking *that* is" if
The lurching or creeping person so indicated
Were crippled or lunatic or winning some dumb bet.
What of *our* walks? yours and mine? All from old Baedekers?

Well, Reinkopf?—*"I suppose that every soul, exiting*
From its crackpot body does an original dance ..."
We dare say that he'd say so. But we two must work out
This matter of ambling, this walking out into things
We have been doing. *Walk* holds *talk* and *work* by their hands,
Between—yet beyond—them both, perplexing the Doctor.
The body's stride and trudge aside, our strolling involves
Our soles and our wingtips equally beating against
The pavements of the pure air and the clouded sidewalks;
Whether gliding through the rainy town on errands of
Light, or idling in some brightened mews at midnight, or
Making the city's great *paseo* late on a fine
Afternoon as shadows beckon to the lights of shops.

Body and Soul

All flesh is as the glass that shatters, through which we see
Within, and cannot do without. Thus as we both gaze
Through this wide pane at the morning haze the ground exhales,
Distant, shrouded mountains and these younger, nearer ones,
Shoulders bared and nudging elbows with each other, all
Seem to paste themselves against another kind of plate,
A pane of air placed between where they are and the glare
That presses its face against this picturing window.
The reflective window meanwhile is half-mirroring
The mind of someone—you? me? or are we of one mind?
—Someone glassy-eyed and starry-minded who surveys
These giant ridges and furrows of thought lit up with
Points of high color where cars crawl along hidden roads.

All glass is as the flesh which refracts its energies
Because of something unseen within it, which is framed
So that the seer and the seen are both beyond it.
Glass through which we look thus reflects our very looking;
So bare limbs embedded in mountain landscape conform
To each other's curving in the body's second thoughts.
Some buried eye of touch peers through the transparency
Of thigh on thigh, hand shaped to breast; this gentle fiction
Lasts a moment only, though: in the next light body
Mirrors body, flesh touches other flesh, by feeling
In touch with itself, as in fables that the clear eye
Whispers to what it can see through, toward what it is out
Of touch with, candid old tales of distance, space and glass.

Behold!

97

No sun shone for so long during that long summer that
Candles everywhere in the land burned with a gray flame.
Gold had become dull, and lead like tar, and the demesne
Of sunny meadows shivered under a foreign reign;
Master craftsmen downed their tools halfway through every piece
Of work, not for enjoyments, but to start on the next
Slightly inferior one; the standard musical
Pitch wandered through a major second from town to town,
And as for numbers, weights and measures—But then you came,
Surveyed the hopeless scene, and, yawning, closed the Big Book
In which all this had been written, shelved it heavily,
And wrote a laughing letter to the whole afternoon
Of great enterprise and beauty (yesterday, this was).

The Old Tale

98

These labor days, when shirking hardly looks like working
Yet sounds far too much like it . . . standing idle, I muse
On which of us two helpmeets, when we weave together,
Is the worker, which, unwittingly, the noisy drone.
Warp might contend with weft for priority, wrecking
The whole frame, wrenching the time into a travesty
Of a day of rest. Were the hum of our shuttling song
Stilled for long, the thin lines strung across the workaday
Loom would sag or snap. But back-and-forth breeds up-and-down:
The figures develop in the field, growing under
The sole working light of our attentiveness. Where would
I be without you? Who ever see you save through me?
United we stand and shake the chains heard round the world.

Back to Town

Once we have grown to a certain size, the very means
By which life is kept in trim come to be those of death;
And for anything larger than a village meeting,
The instruments of the eternal vigilance which
We know must be paid out for liberty are themselves
Chains. So that liberty herself is tithed after all—
A scrap of her drapery, a lock of hair, one more
Wrinkle each minute, filling despair's hope-chest so that
Our freedom may still breathe. How long can this go on? Like
All beautiful creatures must this one too then consume
Herself? Such questions scatter in the light autumnal
Winds, and the point of asking lies buried like a pin,
Hidden, that yet stabs you and cannot be turned away.

The way the hills of Umbria look so movingly
Like their painted versions—a way not of rhyming nor
Translating, let alone of mirroring—had to grow
Up in order to behave like this. Had long ago
To put aside childish things of looking back across
The wide valley through the stony window into the
Widened eye and narrowing gaze of the painter there,
Or of leaping with joy at the sight of its image
—The image of its own mode of resembling—taking
Over from the image of hills, which same had just been
Edging out gold leaf as the stuff out of which backgrounds
Were made. Had to come to where it is, and we are, now:
Our ways our sole high deeds, our roads our destinations.

When our sense of nobility could yet be measured
By a glimpse of a wise Duke appearing plainly at
A window-seat above the courtyard of his handsome
Palace, it was unthinkable that some day the whole
Thing must needs invert—the Duke with his famous profile
Then would sit upon the pot, and the only emblem
Of what in all of us he had once represented
Remained obscure, lurking somewhere in the crowd's catcalls,
In the health just of debunking, the Bronx cheer, the flung
Dung, the mocking jeer with which we hid our sad fear of
Praise, the whipping away of all the old scenery
That was the only act of worshipping left by then.

And then the lusty scorn of noon became the idol
Of the next day. The Scoffer, all sincerity, cast
Hugely in bronze by means of the usual lost wax,
Was raised to that sad eminence in the Plaza, where
The statue to avoid before had been the one of
The local hero, General Whatsisface. *Mocking
Having hardened up into piety, what shall do
The joyful heroic jobs now? What shall represent
Our true Altitude, nobility smuggled within
Its guise? Surely not the old Horseman restored, surely
Not a figure lit by engines of bedazzlement*
—So they wondered, so asked in the privacy of their
Committees, wondering whether to report at all.

What of the Plain Man then, who walked about unadorned
And unadored? He had his brief day, his time of few
Words: "Here's to plain dealing and plain speaking" said the fat
Man; "Mr. Seward, may I have a pen; I'd like to
Do some writing," said the tall one on the train. O, their
Famous fables were pasted up for a goodly while
(Not born aloft by dutiful lictors, nor peering
Through blue greens of waving gonfalons). Those were the days . . .
But what has plain speaking come to? Not a foppishness
Of its own frivolous simplicity—that, one could
Bear—but the long look slowly dropping to the bottom
Line; the flat terrain full of echoes whimpering in
The face of one's dying; complaint as explanation.

There is more to plainness now than the unwrinkled brow
Can reflect. First of all, the work on Simplicity
Being done at the lab out in Evermore has led
To the cracking of the plain; but then, too, the immense
Difficulties in the way of making what was plain
Easy to grasp—the lack of handles that are affixed
Any more firmly than with stickum to the surface,
Any reticulation anchored in something deep—
Made researchers give up the traditional approach.
The plain may be a wild mine of fancy, dancing nymphs
Of trope turning about in (not even below) its
Broadest reaches; flatness full of the creatures of our
Connections; assonance in the silent-growing grass.

—Or it may not: either way, the sense that we can get
Away with skating across the old pond that always
Has been frozen over at our time of year is now
Beset with worries. And the question whether to post
Warnings or not becomes moot when no one around can
Read signs to the littlest of children. Experience
Writes its fables, you may say, in invisible ink,
So that the story-lines of our day-to-day romance
Are unaware of their relation to the text of
The exceptional upon which they comment without
Wisdom, but with some technical skill. If only we
Were simply less than noble! There would be no problem.
General Whatsisface on Horseback would seem sublime.

The thin journalism of our attachments: even
They who write the stuff are seldom caught reading it now.
And it is only when something cannot be given
Away, that the sidewalk vendors start doing just that.
That what the morning brings, then, comes in baker's dozens
Should prove no surprise. It is a little bit extra
That stands for there being a whole lot less than there was:
The gray wheelbarrow full of green and gray ten-dollar
Bills, falling lightly and leafily along the way
To market; the length slowly accruing to shadow
Late in the day when the clock has already been set
Back an hour; what will have been consumed by the time
Harvest has rolled round again, with its great, reddened moon.

Speaking Plainly

For years now we have been getting so used to shoddy
Work, that when something finally comes along that has
Been carefully formed—with pains taken that surfaces
No one will ever see have been finished, and the best
Stuffs used in the old, unimproved-upon ways—we can
Only distrust the whole contraption. Ways of phrasing
Stone, metal, glass, fabric, wood or words that are lazy
About the times, careless of cheap ways we do things now,
Are an overworking of seriousness, labored
Doings in a spontaneous bed. Something too well
Put elicits the sense that something is being put
Over on one. So, lying here, guitar untuned, I
Loosely strum according to the wind, and am believed.

Taking It Easy

When to raise a voice in song was to lay down the law,
Repetitions—even of what once had been commands—
Fell like caresses on us; and those with the dumb ears,
For whom the chant could only drone, danced about the strange
Metal images and spun in the newfangled whirls.
At this the songs grew querulous and once more and yet
Once more corrected the defectors, then fell into
The unyielding ostinato of the paving-stones
Pounded into place, the thudding of sameness, the next
Buttonhole-stitch, the next spot-weld, the next turn of the
Wrench, the labors of love that should rather be its works.
Had not song gone its own wondrous, its own lawless way,
Imperatives would fall on us in joy and beauty.

New Dispensations

Watch the potter as he botches his product, throwing
The piece, that should have been a monument to beauty
Lately banished from symmetry, with a sick motion
Of the wheel, a disturbed caress of the hand, yielding
A tired, ill-shapen lump that falls apart from itself:
So do we mis-shape our lives, inept at Providence.
Watch the welder as he wields the hot allying light,
Sprung from the marriage of foul air and pure, scarring the
Line of the join with the assertive seal of joining
Itself, a rabid priest who weds simple villagers,
Demanding that they take his name: so do we marry
Our seasons, days and years, the flailing blades of our will,
To the great, shaking I-beam. All clatter in the wind.

Watch the besotted glass-blower hiccoughing into
His growing bubble of dream, ay me! the moment of
Involuntary withdrawal of breath, spirit chopped,
Lasts in a brief, bright eternity of crunch preserved,
Of clear globe gone to blast until he crushes the whole
Glassy disaster beneath his heel, and it cuts him:
So do our inspirations fail, all our personal
Crystal worlds smash into gossamer and clear eggshells
At our stuttering of breath, gulpings of our desire;
So do all the consequences of what we do fall
Into some version of the adversary again.
Watch the weak weaver—he knots his yarn into nubbins
Of nastiness: so do we coarsen our every veil.

Watch the carpenter teach an old saw to sing again,
Ripping away along the grain of his pine plank; his
Back-and-forth, his in-and-out of the cleft of the wood,
Lower his blade toward the silences of motionless
Sawdust. Unwisdom's buzz-saw sends us scurrying back
To the self-righteousness of handiwork, the hoarse sound
Of the coughing apothegm that can hold true because
It never meant too much: so do we move back and forth
Again and again, renewing nothing, coming to
The end of the distinction we had drawn in pencil,
To the end of the period we had been sentenced
To serve, to the implication inherent in our
Sawings: the old meaning to which we had been condemned.

Arts and Crafts

In former times all apprenticeship was in itself
Triumphant: the hand of the master lay half-hidden
By, half-glowing through, the nimble enterprise of the
Studio. But that system has long since disappeared.
Indolence, impatience, the whole tax picture, make it
Impossible to get or keep assistants. With each
Man his own master *"Instant Mastery, Now"* is sprayed
Everywhere from cheap paint-cans. So I and my splendid
Apprentices have a secret agreement: Hugh Wood
And Carrie Waters—their very execution is
So brilliant that no one looks beyond that—keep their wise
Peace and silence, content to learn that the better they
Get, the more there is to know; content to outlive me.

Shortage of Help

How can one expect monuments to be preserved when
Even our legally protected dreams crumble to
The dust of half-remembrance? Or all the scale-models
Of places we had loved or feared—O, in a meadow,
Her straw-colored hair interwoven with green, where once
We took cool umbrage at the sun's clearest light, and found
This place, singing with our own desire, yet eternal,
As if topaz-colored rivers flowed out from the land
Around us, as if all other beds and fields would be
Pictures of where we were now, and the embroideries
Of flowering branch worked on our sunny bodies there
Were prefaces to many shadowy verities.
Memory had preserved that private park fairly well.

But when, in want of being in some kind of touch with
Tremblings and glories of an older sort, I intrude
Upon a spot like this in vision, pushing branches
Noisily apart to see her body still embraced
By the green ground, it falls to ruin: there is nothing
But the laughter of the pressed-down grass where she, lying
With her silent and adoring tongue, had lain with me
On a young June afternoon when my breath and hers were
A piece of the general wind. Today, my hearing
Rings with the silent palatal that can make *now* know
Something of *then*: my eyes melt in truth come in sad aid
Of late time: my memory shivers as dark footsteps,
Somewhere, disperse pretty posies laid across her grave.

A Landmark

75

Arachne spies by the door on wise Penelope
To learn what will be her own undoing. By lamplight
She sees the busy shuttle going back on itself
With a more fabulous skill than when, that afternoon,
It had been proudly building the fabric of a shroud.
Taking apart the cover of darkness fabricates
Light, and Time itself goes forward by unravelling:
So the queen's dismembering hand weaves the images
Of faith and remembrance on the bared warp of her loom.
Arachne ignores the lessons of nay-saying that
Lurk in what she sees there in the midnight's unworking.
Her eyes are only for the energies of resolve,
Of what is spun out of oneself in devout silence.

Such emblems of old craftiness that are clear enough
Still to read, point to the one step forward, two-and-a-
Half steps back that everyone eventually gets
Used to. Now you sit on that red prayer-rug, undoing
A dark scarf, skeining the wool in puzzlement, as if
The process should not be still continuing, nature
Having forgotten when to stop, knowing it too well.
But we need not despair of negations: bits of yarn
Snipped far too short for knitting were tied, knot after knot,
Onto the warp and weft of some Anatolian
Frame, shunning all human figures for the intricate
Shapes, "purely decorative," geometric, that lie
Refigured now with shadows of your hands in firelight.

Fancy-Work

Which of these pictures of you shall I keep? An early
Portrait from life? Perhaps the famous scenes, paintings
Done from other pictures for which, in a sense, you "sat"
Far more directly than anyone but I could know.
Or perhaps the old painter's favorite, the somber
Shadowed portrait that he fancied best "either because
He himself was conscious of having failed in it, or
Because others thought he had" (although we would feel more
Comfortable if our own favorite had been his).
I must choose one of them, I who never learned to draw:
What my hand could not manage to project in a plane,
What I can't develop on flat canvas, I shall have
To talk about, to remain a bulky chatterbox.

The Likeness

The wildly-colored girl with her round belly twisted
Further around, as one might twist a plum on its stem
In plucking, her face whacked apart into its aspects,
Steadies the pier-glass full of her reordered image,
Truth having made a mess of false beauty against a
Battlefield of screaming lozenges, all the carnage
Of decoration. Across the gallery the same
Painter allows another, linear, girl to go
Unviolated, guarded by the god of his sad
Heart, a fierce metamorphic beast who caresses her,
Thus warding off the violence that his shining, dark
Eyes would have otherwise commanded an obedient
Brush to execute, as on the girl across the room.

Between these battle-scenes in the wars of figure and
Form, she sits on a low bench and holds up the round glass
In the lid of her compact to her unviolent
Regard. Her tan hand emerges from the gathering
Of the clans of like tone—buff and beige and wheat and bran—
On the plain of what she wears. Beside her, with his hand
Extended to her tan knee as if to steady it,
He has eyes only for hers, she, for the monocled
Gaze of her mirror; yet in these sundry objects each
Espies the object of desire, but invisibly
Disguised as an image of itself. Those two will tear
In time their images, wreck the very subject of
Desire more wildly than whatever the painter wields.

In the Gallery

You must have been peeking at the sketchbook I carried
About last July: it is open to a sheet of
Hopelessly ill-tempered crossings-out; I couldn't catch
Flying scraps of darkness swallowing the summer light.
On the facing page I had had a quick, mute go at
A tranquil pool of bay in the late afternoon fog,
Silence that had to be broken to be remarked on.
You must have seen, too, why I had to give up trying
To draw: the pure syntax with which the great, creating
World is written whispered to me to take up this pen,
Leaving the Faber pencils to someone else, for whom
All those spaces between the letters would silently
Present themselves as figures of deeper lettering.

Thus my refusal to walk beside you with even
A camera nudging my ribs: some pictures taken
Along on our rambles—still lifes, or interiors—
Are aids to reflection, like shades or binoculars.
But taking pictures of wherever we go can serve
Only the spirit of recollection, mother of
Outlines and keeper of the précis. Memorials
Of what we have seen are better made of murmuring
—Ours, and the voluble world's—, by leaving every
Question unanswered, but nobly responded to with
Later questions, whisperings about what was whispered,
Low melodies hummed as the words to the overheard
Tunes of what there is, giving its account of itself.

Travelling Light

122

Here is an old album of wood-engravings—not yours,
But perhaps your sister's—and something neat has been done
To them by way of collage, so that here, for instance,
Sir Roger de Thumpington buggers the chambermaid
Behind the rectory, near a garden-wall where the
Cotton-nightgowned maiden tosses on her half-filled bed,
Or where the vampire is at his hideous repast
Below some casement opened on perilous moonlight.
Tee-hee! But your own pictures are not for laughs—the stretched
White bat in your framed negative, the ardent shadows
Fornicating with the upright streaks of light below
The rucked-up skirts of the old railway arch both amuse
Our high-spirited eyes and instruct our figuring.

In Black and White

123

Where are we now, then? Unable to remain simply
Autumnal any more, what with markets overfull
Of bad red paintings of late afternoon, I locate
My inner weather for you on the map of the year:
Say it is a spell of cold, of chilled nights in the midst
Of a long Indian Summer struck dumb with its own
Fair *longueurs*, dreaming away from what has almost come.
Early autumn looked to be the time of ripening
Truth, and late birds sang of a long moment of shadows
Coming home early to roost in the perches of light.
But the deep, skeptical frost has come and left its first
Hard mark along the surface of the grounds of our hope.
Here is my time, though desire come and go like daylight.

A Time of Year

Remembering my dear dead black cat sometimes returns
Others to my sight—Christine, her kittens Chatto and
Windus (and Fergie), Emmeline and hers, cross Pumpkin,
Bertha of the placid gray, and quiet young Eggplant,
Flora, Bert, nasty Zoltan, Wolfgang and Ludwig's sweet
Mother Priscilla (out of whom by Wilson they were);
Where are the Others' cats I knew—Georgia, Maisie, Wow
(Of these only noble Rose remains). Where are they now?
And where are all their days, the yesteryears and images
That melt like black snow along a dark, familiar rug?
Furred felicities absent them from us in a while;
Months ago I'd promised you something for poor Wolfgang:
What can be said of dead cats that is not dead itself?

What can be said of dead cats? That is not dead itself
Which can escape the icy caress of accurate
Memory (and, you might add, make her stuffy, bemused
Daughters buzz off); come help me then with some fancy-work
(Like all cats I have known he belonged also to you):
A corona for Wolfgang now all of evergreen
Intertwined with catnip which would send him and Ludwig
(His poor gray brother who predeceased him by not quite
A year) literally up the wall. But you must pluck
Faded souvenirs like that figuratively out
Of this wreath lest it wither now like last summer's news.
There can be no catalogue of habits, or times when ...
No contrived inventory of storied occasions.

No contrived inventory of storied occasions
Could record the string of being holding them in line,
The part of whatever room it was that for a time
Became the place of the cat, lair, veld, branch, hearth or crag.
And yet now—even with your forefinger at my lips—
I reform unutterable losses, reaffirm
What I was making of him alive. Dead now a year,
He is in my hands; I feel him draped around my neck,
Hear the all-but-silent fall of paw on midnight floor,
Drops of some tincture of the Absolute. Absence breeds
Presences in the cells it hollows out in the rock
Of our days, and I can't wonder how, in shudders of
Remembering, my dear dead black cat sometimes returns.

Requiescat

127
___

Images of place that loss commanded one to set
Up—the bright beach, the cold hills, the meadow, the pinewoods—
Wait about the available nearby space, open
To any visitors, until nightfall, when, folded
Home, they loll more easily about, no longer prey
To misdevotion, but gentle idles of the page.
And yet now, having got wind of you, the crowds of pines
Stir into assertion; the hills whistle through their rocks;
The beach conjoins its own interpretive roars. And thus
It is they who address themselves, not to images
Of absence such as they had been, but to a presence:
They who have been spoken vainly to and falsely of
In too many chilly idylls now resound in truth.

Remembering Where

128
___

P works on his uncommissioned portrait of the world
Shed of figments, his brush giving substance and taking
Cover from the winter scene which cannot warm to it.
A self-portrait of the face of nature has long since
Been worked up on the artless surface of his pallette.
The dry noises of underpainting are nothing to
The loud solitude of a world unable to come
Together with images of itself. The clouded
Meaning of a sky that P had supposed would speak for
The glimmering, blank land that lay below was silent.
And that land, unclothed even in a light shift of snow,
Lay bare in herself: shivering nakedly though, or
Free of the fabric of dream? Unknowing P daubs on.

Plein-air

The language of the howling wind allows an endless
Tale of winter to be told in one long syllable,
Here where this sea of flowing air has become a mere
Glaring of diffuse and mindless light, as unaware
As each dumb, chilling mid-day is of its transience,
Of how it will be grasped by the comprehensive dark.
Everything we see in such light is an optical
Allusion, and not to the winter of sunny noons,
Of smooth-packed snow gleaming in the farmyard, icicles
Eyeing the ground under the barn, of the white shed where
A dairymaid still churns by hand away at the tub
Of metaphor. Not to that, but to the fact-ridden
Land of the unfair cold space, of the unblinking time.

Grounds of Winter

After the midwinter marriages—the bride of snow
Now of one body with the black ground, the ice-heiress
Bedded with her constant rock, the far hills of one mind
With the bare sky now, and the emperor of rivers
Joined with the most recent of his flowing concubines—
After the choirs of the cold have died on the late air,
Low now as our unagitated humdrum heartbeats
Still go about their irreversible chores again,
You and I have heard the song of the long afterword:
The phrases of the moon crooning to the fields below,
The cracking language of frozen forests whose summer
Harps were long since smashed, and the profound, recurrent vow
This bright stream's soft echoing answer rings to the woods.

Metathalamia

Cras amet qui nunquam amavit, quiquam amavit cras
Moriatur—"those who never loved before will love
Tomorrow; those used to loving will tomorrow come
To die"—The old refrains all come down to this: either
Reduced to *tra-la-las*, at whose regular return
Children look at each other and, smiling, mouth the words
And old people nod heads in time, or, if they retain
Meaning at all, they always end up in whispering
"*Death*" in the deep chambers hidden in among their tones.
That is how *Greensleeves*, her smock stained from love in the grass,
Outlasts all the boys who had a go at her. That is
How *nonny-nonny-no* etcetera can survive
The next stanza, and the next, and the next, and the next.

Breaking off the song of the refrain, putting the brakes
On the way that the ever-returning chorus tends
To run away with the whole song—well, that may well be
Breaking away from a frightening joyride before
The wrap-up of metal around some tree or other.
Yes, you say, *but something has to get out of hand so*
That we can go on: and, yes, I answer, but better
Let it be the new material in each stanza
That bridles at sense, reckless of disaster, and leaps
Up into the less and less trustworthy air. The same
Old phrase comes back anyway, waiting for what we say
To be over and done, marking its time, the heavy
Burden of the tune we carry, humming, to the grave.

Refrains

Old iambic ways of walking helped us amble past
Look-alikes among the flowers, telling them apart;
Objects contemplated for their singleness remained
Clear of how our thought objects to such naïve beliefs
As in flowers-in-themselves; and powers that subject
Nature so impressively to notice and to long
Memory themselves are subjects of the Empress Mind.
But our fluid, modern stride drowns outlines of nouns and
Verbs in its impatience. Subject of my thoughts, object
Of my desire, knower and the known, run together
On flattened paths. You and I hold hands across our verbs
Of being: who then is subject, who object? Do not
Think I quibble! This is a matter of mind and world.

Our Distress

M's verses (wrote the boring lady bard now dead) smelled
Of the lamp; and aside from how they are still fragrant
With day, with night, with the many subordinating
Twilights, the lady knew little of the ways of lamps:
Tallow on the white bear's fur east of the sun and west
Of the moon; oil from Psyche's trembling hand; the cold blue
Light cupped in the sconces on the walls of hell that showed
The dear, careful brow of Eurydice traversing,
Behind one, the rocky way up and out (let alone
The kind of lamp that burns eight days on one evening's oil);
The metallic smell of my small flashlight sweeping out
Pale demonstrations in the sky of the summer night
That awakened my wide, thirteen-year-old longing eye.

The ways of lamps are dark, their light guarded by shadows:
Would one have had M write by moonlight, then?—that had been
Bottled for bedroom use long before the lady bard
Was born. All of which brings me to this matter of light:
The old study-lamp you brought me long ago, its cocked
Head looking with an inner light at the opened page
Of Alpha's welcoming gaze, or Beta's turning back,
Or Gamma's belly, or Delta's triangle of fur
Where soft portals have been touched by adoring hands of
Shadow, or solemn Epsilon's hand in hand of mine.
As hot as it is bright; sun, moon and constellations
That guide our works and nights, your lamp smells of M's poems, yes,
And all the other nifty redolences of the world.

Lady with the Lamp

Your softened shadow now when you come up quietly
Behind me, falls across the place where I am, and most
Particularly cancels the sharper-edged, dark grey
Shadow, dancing irritably, of my writing hand,
Which swallows up the first letters of these very words
Even as I write them out now, so that, in them, *"the—"*
Emerges into light on the left only as *"—m"*
Lies buried in the handy darkness surrounding its
Generation. But that your shade is like light itself
Making clear the story of starting up and ending,
I might have thought that this shading of hurried letters
Was your work, taking back what you knew to have been yours
Of what, here by lamplight, I thought to originate.

Replevin

"It's a long lane that has no turning": Comment upon
This saying—the written part of an entrance exam
Taken long ago produced I don't remember what
Kind of bluster from me about how a small "indeed,"
After the first word, would help the syntax out a lot.
Construing comes first; then putting wrong constructions on
The hoary old rightnesses had better claim our time.
Very well, then: The very long lane, the longest one,
Has indeed no turning, narrowed so that two cannot
Pass at one time, stretching further out than all desire.
(Longing is short enough: having at last is nothing,
Or even less than nothing—loss. For which, witness the
Brevity of soul, and darkness's longevity.)

The Long Lane

138

Unanswered, our riddles remain wise and beautiful
In their impossibility of is and is-nots, ones
And manys at once, fluctuating numbers of legs.
The Gordian knot was gorgeous if you stopped to look.
Solving them shoots down the angels of their oddity,
And the prize that thunks down on the hard ground at one's feet
Might as well have been store-bought. One must always recall
The puzzle in the elusive thrumming of its flight,
Or be left with garbage. Like the punned and anagrammed
Crossword, finally finished on that scrap of magazine:
What's it good for now? Eating a ripe peach on? Fold it
Up into a paper airplane, send it flying out
A window of the city, raising questions anew.

Being Puzzled

139

Unless the green traffic-light were reduced by my crude,
Narrowing regard to a cold eye of permission,
Pursuers would honk like geese in fury, and rightly
So. Unless the red always dutifully remained
A button pushing into my centers of arrest,
There would be crashes and much expensive body-work.
But unless, at least three times a day, that disc of green
Did not demand that its fables be unfolded, that
One wonder what kind of boundless color of ocean
On a fine day poured into a broth of the tinctures
Of grasses and fir—boughs—that its particular green
Lose that dumb tone of command—then what? Then nothing: there
Would be no engine at all worth pampering with gas.

Go Ahead

"Flat Parnassus, super-highway, carrying your freight
Of fact, such as that I am here and that she is there,
That each mile I move toward her may bring me no closer
To the end of longing"—so I sang as the long band
Of road unrolled, fringed with all the emblems of my flight:
Socony's Pegasus flew by in scarlet, Tydol's
Wingèd *A* showed that the letter outflew the spirit,
The golden Shell of pilgrimage openly gave up
The highway's echoed roar to my obedient ears.
My heart was in images of the West—I, buried
In the heart of the East, drawn by film after gray film
To the dust-stung ruins of our far deserts, before
The roads opened up for business and closed down for song.

Highway, 1949

My musings on your past have been filled more than once with
An ancient friend of yours, that lover of horses and
Of a far star, who studied, fought and sang, and yet scrawled
Philippics against his own encroaching self, raising
The citizenry of his soul to bear arms against
Bare arms and pale thighs denied him when his bright star fell
From the sky into a rich marriage with someone else.
He could not refrain from bridling at the groom, but all
That stuff of intricate muttering and blunt quibble
Kept the lost lady's name alight among the hosts of
Inconsiderate stars. With us, quite the opposite—
Your undying name preserves my mortal one: my work
Carves out the room for your memorializing play.

An Old Beau

Maurice Scève found the tomb of Petrarch's Laura, but not
On the sacred ground of the Vaucluse, as the book says:
In the stony figure of his own fictive lady
Of delight, there was the grave of Laura, where she lay.
Asteria Stern—the little girl whose gentle neck
And lovingly twisted braid of hair showing over
The back of the schoolroom chair broke my heart—her clear eyes
Entombed no Delia for Delia had never
Lived; but gazing at her image in my bed, squinting
Through longing's archaic astrolabe, I could learn of
The parallax by which that image was centered in
My field of vision alone: "Stern? Yuck!" (in fact, its then
Equivalent), jeered the silly boys in the schoolyard.

What you have gathered from our talks of Asteria
Stern and the others, then, enables you to propound
Not one more monument, not to build or yet become
Yourself a bit of statuary, but a theory
Of entombment, a walking meditation upon
All memorials, a grammar of storage. So that
When, my hands full of the task-crammed moment, I send you
To the broad, autumnal shelves for something to leave through,
What you come up with always changes in your quiet
Grasp, quickens with all of what it had been meant for it
To become: old star-maps revised in your afternoon
Eyelight; dust blown smilingly from heavy folios,
Joining the stellar whirl of possible golden motes.

Seeing Stars

We say that fact yields truth. But how? mindlessly, as fields
Their crop of grass? hastily, as blackened underbrush
Its rush of blueberries? or reluctantly, as a
Surly guard hands over prisoners to the bearer
Of the great Emperor's seal? But there is this yielding:
In among careless weeds and boring, necessary
Perennials, out of the foul but hopeful magma
Of what indeed it falls to us all to be and do—
Pain, irritation, tedium, rage, sly childishness,
Longing, despair amid the bad weather and the good—
Out of all this muck the particular plant springs forth,
Like a laughing nymph appearing out of the green bank
Of one's own secret river: what the place had been for.

Suppose this were a sprig of myrtle: from what tears, sweat
And wrinkled, ungardened beds does she spring? Dear Olive
And famous but weary Laurel grow here, labelled with
Their names and histories, and were I a husbandman
Of garlands I'd lay out Myrtle whose deepening green
Crowns all our couplings and shades all our passionate beds.
Yet she would end up like all the others: "Look for truth
Not in the dusty books, but in her eyes" Or "Seek not
To penetrate the eastern mysteries, but enter
Her and be truly wise" Or "Myrtle's motion beneath
Your body's hot doings makes the world turn" "Her cry of
Coming will sound for eternity in the long halls
Of desire." Like the others, Myrtle's one for the books.

Grounds and Beliefs

92

Suppose that you had laid me under an injunction
Never once to utter the syllable of your name;
My soon-to-be-ritualized circumlocution
—*Why, Oh You?*—would always be perforce a questioning,
Not about the nature of your name, but of your will
And the necessities it imposed on my discourse
And, thereby (in the ways I still keep trying over
And over again to explain), on yours. Yet suppose
I called you simply *U*, the twenty-first letter, (*I*
Being the ninth one—both factored by the three of us,
I, you, and the abyss unmarked by any letter).
Even adding this aught to what is, I figure now
To end up with a knowledge of just what I owe you.

Promissory Note

Why do I write you notes in this funny line, long, like
Proletarian fourteeners marching in their way;
Or like the alexandrine, split into groups of three
Beats; or else falling in anapests patterned in fours;
Or else partaking of the noble ten who marched in
Pairs of lines like fighting-men advancing on the words
Of disarray—even the various guerrillas,
Sniping at the phalanxes and squares of orderly
Procession, or moving in jagged—not ragged—lines
Waving bibles like banners, yea, brandishing scripture,
Against old dispensations: like these, unlike them, too,
In that inaudibly marching and dancing loudly
Are both covered by its mandate to be of itself?

Well, the questions of discourse, if drawn out long enough,
Start answering themselves; and yet the point is not
Why you of all people should merit a tone whose own
Clang, whose essential ground, lies both in what it is like
And what unlike—all that is merely personal, as if,
Say, I always kidded you in a Yiddish accent
Sounding as from as close to Wilno as I could feign.
No, the question should be what to make of the way that
Lengths of wordage from the various times of the day—
Questions and answers, puzzle-games, prayers, quarrels and songs—
Of "doubt, desire or emotion," the old standards of love—
Should at night, of themselves, come to stand in quiet lines
Like these, to be recounted, embraced and led to bed.

An Apology for Poetry

149

In the repeating calendar of regret, I turn
A page and find an anniversary: every day,
Every very day comes to another's summoning.
What was happening, then, on, say, 6/6/66?
It was my last summer in this calm town, and before
Leaving, I sat that month and fussed with picture-puzzles
On a quiet back porch—it was one of those warm days
Like 7/7/77, in the first
Summer of returning here, when I sat on a far
Longer porch, numbering some unfallen leaves. Still here,
In this sad town, I sum up such moments now for the
Reckoning day of a month beyond, pervading all
Mere months, where it is always 13/13/13.

Today's Date

150

A day I had forgotten reappeared to me, clad
In a kind of dimmed radiance, neither presenting
Its case, nor yet asking me to represent my own,
But with an equitable air went on its errand
Of merely being there. I called out for you to come
And help me deal with it, but you were somewhere else (out
Looking across the morning water at where the next
Morning would be coming from, it now appears you were).
So that pale day waited, and on being asked in which
Of the volumes of my life it was to be inscribed,
Disappeared with the curious perfume and the most
Melodious twang so common to such vanishings.
That was when you came in with a flaming day-lily.

That's for Oblivion

Where were you back in New York in nineteen forty-two?
The World War won, the Second One then in the winning,
I left one kind of boyhood for its starved antitype.
I still got you mixed up with the genius loci
Of some timely spot, as in nineteen fifty-five when
Rain made Harvard brickwork glisten, my mind drank the light.
Back in New York again in 'sixty-eight, even then
We had met with some kind of recognition, although
I still went my own hasty way too much of the time.
Yet again in Connecticut, my fifty-second
Year is in your hands—and you in mine—who commanded
Candles of ardent occasion to deepen their glow,
Turning nights of passage into moments of lustre.

Lustra

You wrote something on this page last summer. I've just come
Across it. Trying to make sense of it now, trying
To figure out what the errand was you might have sent
Me on—and, even more, what new chore knowing about
What you'd meant then sets up for me now—it's like coping
With the Law that, while being laid down, had been cut up
Into bits with some sort of saw. Thus the commandment
Was to interpret before all else. The puzzling
Injunctions, cross words, prohibitions themselves riddled
With gaps that might or not be loopholes, are more binding
Than bronze statutes standing in public squares, stone tables
Set up in rocky precincts, too easily followed
To have to be obeyed. More binding. More to be sung.

Stories are a matter, though, of radiance, of wholes.
Thus: The day was too clear and bright merely to have been
Exemplary, to blossom and then blast with sundown
And subsequent decay into the mud of the night,
Into one more bit of what could not be *evidence*
That the sun also rises etcetera. The day
Was too clearly that day—when you laughed over spilt milk,
When I cried over spilt wine, when we saw eagles, claw
Hooked in claw, wheeling together over the bald crags—
To be merely that, or to be merely a July
Someteenth. That it was a day like any other meant
That it was totally singular, a story too
Clear, too directly told not to be a parable.

Last Summer

You rely on what I say about you (as do I).
You use me for my purposes I'm ignorant of.
You are given to utter what I must intimate.
You are the Urtext: I have done the illustrations.
You are the ultramarine in which I am enisled.
You are ultimate: I'm intermediate, and so
If you are Ithaca then I must be Ulysses;
I roam indiscriminately toward your urgent shore,
I learn inductively what is understood for you.
I improvise over your recurring undersong.
In and out my mind moves while you have your ups and downs.
I illuminate the darkness that you usher in.
I am a bad liar: you are as good as your word.

You and I

Locked up in this cell as if in punishment for some
Transgression, I pace out daily the determined ground
Between walls of very old stone, knowing no one else
Has ever been kept here. To temper my loneliness
In this room's vast tract of time, I summon up some past
Prisoners, imagine their ancient graffiti here:
"XIII—Atlas holds the sky up, three Hesperides
Stand by in admiration" chiseled on one bare wall
Speaks for a shaping spirit; some figuring one rhymes
"My pent-up thoughts I'll fix, till I have served my time, on
Fibonacci number six which is the seventh prime."
These fancy up the fact of time, while I try to learn
Words of the language in which you'll hand me my parole.

Too Much Freedom

Triskaidekaphobia across the centuries
Kept us seating one more at the table, even when
The extra one was silly or redundant or gross.
Moreover, the new arrangements—the sexes paired off,
The doubled sevens, the mysteries of ten and four—
Masqueraded as reasons, hiding always our fear
Of dangerous and pungent oddments behind the bright
And interesting arrangements that terror had us make.
Like grownups now, allowing the black cats to amble
Across our shadows in the forenoon without alarm,
We can at least, in a poor time for discourse, invite
Exactly whom we please, whom we need: it will be right
In a new shape, finished beyond the old completions.

But then, you say, we go on talking at dinner for
A longer time these days: yes, it too runs over the
Edge of what might have been both decent and effective.
Fine cooking makes one talk of remembered meals; beyond
That there is gossip of the harmless kind, overtures
Toward attractive persons, narratives (the payment of
What one is dining out on) and all the rest of it
That cushions, as in claret velvet, the glittering
Truth that one of us startles the rest by propounding.
We do go on . . . but dinner is our serious meal
—Light lunch is not—and even knowing that where we sit
Lingering over drink is at the edge of something
Dreadful soon to happen makes it worth talking about.

In all fairness, when the reasonable noon's blond head
Stretches out along the grass outside our living-room,
In the light of all this, we must remember how once
Loki looked into the place on Valhalla where twelve
Were feasting, added one more, and that was Balder's last
Lunch. On Friday, too. And later on, when there should have
Been only, at the disordered *seder*, the Leader
(Who said: "This is the Bread of Affliction—that's me!—which
Was rushed through its baking on the way out of darkness")
And the Eleven, there was the One more who would help
Make it all twelve again for a while, until they all
Fell one by one, knowing how they had been reclining
On dangerous ground, in the foul shadow of thirteen.

An anniversary cannot be an occasion
Solemn enough any more for breaking out the last
Of the old wine: they have got at yearly intervals
The way they have at public statues, and a private
Moment—a death, a birth, a passage into the next
Chamber that had been awaiting your arrival—has
Been nationalized by the commissars of twelvemonth
So that even the year, to a day, when I first saw
You take form against a background of shadows in that
Room we know so well—even that day has become trash,
Might as well have been proclaimed National Every Day.
Let us drink instead, then, touching glasses, kissing wine
To the memory of tonight last year a month ago.

I heard a rumor that you had dreamed of a New Home
Found by wandering through the mazes of an old one
—A big house in which you were small long summers ago—
Returning to it yearly in dream, and dream of dream,
And then one day in one night's dreaming coming upon
A place where one's bed was, and more: a chamber in which
You handed over your arms, your armor, at the door
Because you did not want them there; a place you never
Hankered after, because when you were away from it
The memory of it dissolved in a solution
Of feeling. That was what bred desire, not for it but
For the someone elses. In your dream you knew this was
The Room of the Thirteen, odd and unaccountable.

But this may yield something: say the room had to be "of"
Some prime, and yet some prime fresh from the barrel, as it
Were, uncomplicated by the ordinary sets
It was the undying cardinal of: *Eleven*,
Even, conjures up The Winning Throw, or strategies
Of passes, high goals, penetrations, backs in motion
—Your room was not about that, though perhaps about what
All that gaming for such long stakes itself was about.
So: the first prime number unattached to meaning, though
Shaded a bit with meaningless fear—at most, fear that
It had no meaning—that was the number of The Room.
Enough, now, lest we both learn that your dream repainted
A number on the door that had been *One*. Or *Zero*.

At thirteen already single-minded Abraham
Smashed up all the idols in his father's house that were
Likenesses of nothing, and turned his inner eye toward
The Lord of Nonrepresentation, whose sole image
Lies encoded somewhere in our own. So at thirteen,
Boys with minds aswim are called up out of their Third World
To sing the old law aloud from an opened scroll, to
Stand up and be counted, and yet more: to count themselves
Fortunate and wise in not coming of age at twelve
Or ten or twenty (months, toes and fingers keeping those
Accounts) but at a time whose number, even more odd,
Signifies its own solitariness and whose square
(One sixty-nine years old?) breeds doubt ("I should live so long!")

Just the right number of letters—half the alphabet;
Or the number of rows on this monument we both
Have to share in the building of. We start out each course
Now, of dressed stone, with something of me, ending where you
Handle the last block and leave something of you within
Or outside it. So we work and move toward a countdown,
Loving what we have done, what we have left to do. A
Long day's working makes us look up where we started from
And slowly to read down to the end, down to a base,
Not out, to some distant border, the terminal bland
Destructions at their ends that lines of time undergo.
Endings as of blocks of text, unlit by the late sun
Really underlie our lives when all is said and done.

Is it the plenitude of seasons, then, the number
Of weeks each one must have for its full hand of cards, that
Gives us a sense of its completeness? The seasons sit
Around the annular table each holding a pure
Run: Winter wields only the spades, Summer brandishes
Hot, black clubs, Spring showers hearts about and Autumn shows
A fall of diamonds in our climate of extremes.
Our parents in Eden, deathless, parentless, were dealt
The perfect year's full hand of intermingled weeks when
Continual spring and fall scattered variations
Of face and number in among the months, whose first names
Were merely decorative. Now seasons play for keeps:
Death deals, and cheats with the false promise of final trumps.

Not for this dull blue, the humdrum stars there to be read
In rows that accrue over the years, but for the quite
Original, true number of stripes which since have bred
Such a changing crew of constellations, was the height
At which the flag flew appropriate and merited.
The oddly-placed hue that tells us to stop is set right
Against tracks of highest clattering overhead.
Windy harp of thirteen strings, a Cretan lyre that might
Descant upon its own fabrications! yet, folded
Away, dreaming of signals from A to Z all night
(Or, as the double-crossed Union Jack would say, "to Zed").
Ensign of life where only interstices are white:
Mud, low sunlight, blood, we begin and end in the red.

Crazy Hans sits on the sidewalk strumming his crazy
Guitar—he has carefully re-fretted the whole thing
And fussed with every string so that touches of sour
Harmony fumble their way into the evening air.
But in his less-than-semi-tones a silent order
Reigns; every unrhyming triad has its reasons
For sounding off as it does: in his thirteen-tone scale
Of falsifications the octaves alone are true.
The blues he sings, confusing in the strings with the hues
And cries of the sidewalk, wraps them all up in a roll
Of night. A chorus totally of blue notes enfolds
The random airs of the corner where he sits strumming.
Crazy Horst across the street roars to his own tom-tom.

At last, the clock has struck thirteen. It would be too late,
Even if that were the matter, to get the clock fixed.
But it rings true and in its way is right twice a day:
Soon after noon it strikes our moment, the time you come
To find me at a table by the window, whereon
Ripening fruit, a thoughtful jug, an uncrumpled cloth
Receiving the shadows can compose a *nature morte*
That is somehow still life, still part of the world of breath.
The clock rings in your arrival, making room in time
For our dear discourse in all its hidden silences,
Room in time among the hurried hours that shoulder
Each other into the cold, dim valley at the end
Of day and night where they shall ever stand shuddering.

That other time of day when the chiming of Thirteen
Marks the hour in truth comes after midnight has made
Its unseen appearance. Then the whole trembling house starts
Gathering itself together in sudden fear, creaks
On the stairs grow tacit, and, even outside, the wind
In the lindens has been hushed. Unlike the time beyond
Noon, when your visitations shape that original
Hour, when we pull the shades down in our space between
Moments totally contiguous in the clocked world,
This black gap between days is no place for us: should you
Creep into my bed then you would find me shuddering
As at the opening of a secret whose shadowed
Power unbroken lay in coupling day unto day.

Thirteen

Let me say first that, although in the demanding light
Of morning the discrepancies rattling our discourse
Speak of a noisier afternoon, what can be heard
Is the sound of things evening up between our two
Conditions—as if we were light and sound disputing
Claims for primacy at the morning of the world; till
The odd, evening hour, neither yours nor mine, but ours,
When our hands reach out to touch like object and image
Moving toward the mirror's surface each through the magic
Space that the other's world must needs transform in order
To comprehend; when our voices have surrounded one
Another, each like some penumbra of resonance.
So that you have the last word now I give it to you.

At the End of the Day

From Blue Wine

BLUE WINE

for Saul Steinberg

1

The winemaker worries over his casks, as the dark juice
Inside them broods on its own sleep, its ferment of dreaming
Which will turn out to have been a slow waking after all,
All that time. This would be true of the red wine or the white;
But a look inside these barrels of the azure would show
Nothing. They would be as if filled with what the sky looks like.

2

Three wise old wine people were called in once to consider
The blueness of the wine. One said: "It is 'actually' not
Blue; it is a profound red in the cask, but reads as blue
In the only kind of light that we have to see it by."
Another said: "The taste is irrelevant—whatever
Its unique blend of aromas, bouquets, vinosities
And so forth, the color would make it quite undrinkable."
A third said nothing: he was lost in a blue study while
His eyes drank deeply and his wisdom shuddered, that the wine
Of generality could be so strong and so heady.

3

There are those who will maintain that all this is a matter
Of water—hopeful water, joyful water got into
Cool bottles at the right instant of light, the organized
Reflective blue of its body remembered once the sky
Was gone, an answer outlasting its forgotten question.
Or: that the water, colorless at first, collapsed in glass
Into a blue swoon from which it never need awaken;
Or: that the water colored in a blush of consciousness
(Not shame) when it first found that it could see out of itself
On all sides roundly, save through the dark moon of cork above
Or through the bottom over which it made its mild surmise.

There are those who maintain this, they who remain happier
With transformations than with immensities like blue wine.

4

He pushed back his chair and squinted through the sunlight across
At the shadowy, distant hills; crickets sang in the sun;
His mind sang quietly to itself in the breeze, until
He returned to his cool task of translating the newly
Discovered fragments of Plutarch's lost essay "On Blue Wine."
Then the heavy leaves of the rhododendrons scratched against
Gray shingles outside, not for admittance, but in order
To echo his pen sighing over filled, quickening leaves.

5

"For External Use Only?" Nothing says exactly that,
But there are possibilities—a new kind of bluing
That does not whiten, but intensifies the color of,
All that it washes. Or used in a puzzle-game: "Is blue
Wine derived from red or white? emerging from blood-colored
Dungeons into high freedom? or shivering in the silk
Robe it wrapped about itself because of a pale yellow chill?"
One drink of course would put an end to all such questioning.

6

". . . and when he passed it over to me in the dim firelight,
I could tell from the feel of the bottle what it was: the
Marqués de Tontada's own, *El Corazón azul*. I had
Been given it once in my life before, long ago, and
I tell you, Dan, I will never forget the moment when
It became clear, before those embers, that the famous blue
Color of the stuff could come to mean so little, could change
The contingent hue of its significance: the truer
To its blue the wine remained, the less it seemed to matter.
I think, Dan, that was what we had been made to learn that night."

7

This happened once: Our master, weary of our quarreling,
Laughed at the barrel, then motioned toward us for a drink; and
Lo, out of the sullen wooden spigot came the blue wine!

III

8

And all that long morning the fair wind that had carried them
From isle to isle—past the gnashing rocks to leeward and around
The dark vortex that had been known to display in its whorls
Parts not of ships nor men but of what it could never have
Swallowed down from above—the fair wind blew them closer to
The last island of all, upon the westernmost side of
Which high cliffs led up to a great place of shining columns
That reddened in the sunset when clouds gathered there. They sailed
Neither toward this nor toward the eastern cape, darkened by low
Rocks marching out from the land in raging battle with the
Water; they sailed around a point extending toward them, through
A narrow bay, and landed at a very ancient place.
Here widely-scattered low trees were watching them from the hills.
In huge casks half-buried there lay aging the wine of the
Island and, weary half to madness, they paused there to drink.
This was the spot where, ages before even their time, Bhel
Blazed out in all his various radiances, before
The jealousy of Kel led to his being smashed, as all
The old tales tell, and to the hiding and the parceling
Out of all the pieces of Bhel's shining. Brightness of flame,
Of blinding bleakness, of flavescent gold, of deepening
Blush-color, of the shining black of obsidian that
Is all of surface, all a memory of unified
Light—all these were seeded far about. There only remained
The constant fraction, which, even after every sky
Had been drenched in its color, never wandered from this spot.
And thus it was: they poured the slow wine out unmingled with
Water and saw, startled, sloshing up against the insides
Of their gold cups, sparkling, almost salty, the sea-bright wine . . .

9

It would soon be sundown and a shawl of purple shadow
Fell over the muttering shoulders of the old land, fair
Hills and foul dales alike, singing of noon grass or Spanish
Matters. The wooden farmhouses grew grayer and the one
We finally stopped at, darker than the others, opened its
Shutters and the light inside poured over the patio.
Voices and chairs clattered: we were welcomed and the youngest

Child came forth holding with both hands a jug of the local wine.
It was blue: reality is so Californian.

10

Under the Old Law it was seldom permitted to drink
Blue wine, and then only on the Eight Firmamental
Days; and we who no longer keep commandments of that sort
Still liked to remember that for so long it mattered so
Much that they were kept. And thus the domestic reticence
In my family about breaking it out too often:
We waited for when there was an embargo on the red,
Say, or when the white had failed because of undue rain.
Then Father would come up from the cellar with an abashed
Smile, in itself a kind of label for the dark bottle.
At four years old I hid my gaze one night when it was poured.

11

Perhaps this is all some kind of figure—the thing contained
For the container—and it is these green bottles themselves,
Resembling ordinary ones, that are remarkable
In that their shapes create the new wines—*Das Rheinblau, Château
La Tour d'Eau, Romanée Cerulée*, even the funny old
Half-forgotten *Vin Albastru*. And the common inks of
Day and night that we color the water with a drop of
Or use for parodies of the famous labels: these as
Well become part of the figuring by which one has put
Blue wine in bold bottles and lined them up against the light
There in a window. When some unexpected visitor
Drops in and sees these bottles of blue wine, and does not ask
At the time what they mean, he may take some drops home with him
In the clear cup of his own eye, to see what he will see.

AUGUST CARVING

Your file which whispers against the piece of silent limestone,
Urging a pair of joined figures into the life of light,
Is echoing the crickets working away at the air
This side of the far cornfield. The cornfield itself mirrors
Something very distant, some place of green, some steadfastness.
The figures coming into stone being commemorate
Our consciousness of bodies' joining, a knowledge as of
Distant light composed here by the green of fields, distant stone
Echoed in these gray blocks resting in the afternoon grass.
The stone pair have been making love but that is as nothing:
The he and she celebrate the embrace of light and stone.
Light will fall from them, as from ourselves: they will pass among
Moments of astonishing shadow, then enter the dark,
Coldly, invisibly, forms fractured from their radiance.

SOME OF THE PARTS

In the assurance of oncoming twilight that there is
A vast, pliable space containing regions of our life
That keep entirely in touch, day and night will not crack
Apart. The light on the cold grass will leave slowly, rising
Out of sight, and its claim on colors will be relinquished.
All surfaces will tacitly assent to this. The shell
Of night will start singing into the ear of the day's shell,
And they will have been washed in the one sea that is all depth
And no surface, yea, even like the little pond dwelling
Off in the near corner of the audible world, waveless,
Bottomless, but brimming with an encouraging chorus
Of sounding night. Remembering which, in the swarm of noon's
Tiny-winged exigencies, will flake apart the promise
Of it, lying in the sun like the pieces of some dream.

From Spectral Emanations

Spectral Emanations

A Poem in Seven Branches in Lieu of a Lamp

"*There was a meaning and purpose in each of its seven branches, and such a candlestick cannot be lost forever. When it is found again, and seven lights are kindled and burning in it, the whole world will gain the illumination which it needs. Would not this be an admirable idea for a mystic story or parable, or seven-branched allegory, full of poetry, art, philosophy, and religion? It shall be called 'The Recovery of the Sacred Candlestick.' As each branch is lighted, it shall have a differently colored lustre from the other six; and when all seven are kindled, their radiance shall combine into the white light of truth.*"

The golden lamp of the Second Temple in Jerusalem, borne into Rome in the triumph of Titus, probably did not fall off the Milvian bridge when Constantine saw in the sky the sign by which he would conquer. The text which follows intends to hoist up another lamp from other waters than those of the Tiber. Lost bronze is silent, let alone lost gold; even the newest oil has no echo. I have here kindled the lights of sound, starting with the red cry of battle, followed by the false orange gold, true yellow goldenness, the green of all our joy, blue of our imaginings, the indigo between and the final violet that is next to black, for that is how our scale runs. Below each cup of color is a branch of prose, following and supporting it. Only at the moment of green is there time for a story, for only that branch is vertical, the other supports being parabolic. This is in memory of my father,
Franklin Hollander, 1899–1966.

PROLOGUE

THE WAY TO THE THRONE ROOM

On the captive shore, the bright river hard by, this happened:
I had seen what I had seen, and I had come to the gates.

At the gate, questions were put. As: *Who poured the oil?
Penemue,* I allowed, *the breather inside. He who taught
me to know the bitter from the sweet, and how to write
with ink and paper.*

As: *Who trimmed the wick? Gananiel,* I confessed, *the lopper
of branches, the one who limits that the many may flourish. Surely he did it.*

As: *Who struck a light? Bhel,* I reconstructed, *the starred one,
that we may see, that we may write our poor books, white
fire on black fire.*

As: *Who kindled the flames? Puriel,* I suggested, *the melter
and blender who cast the cups of fiery gold and then
cupped the golden fire.*

As: *Who raised his hands toward the burning? Why, Roy G.
Biv,* I snorted, *the man of lead, though his melting point
was low, Roy G. Biv.*

As: *Who wept at the light? O, I did,* I chanted, *or at least I
did when I remembered the radiance.*

As: *Who ended it all? Dr. Hitson, the awakener,* I screamed,
*he blew out the flames at the end—with an explosion of
violent force.*

Then I halted at the cold gates. Statues waited at wide intervals along the courtyard, disposed in flexions of the usual; their faces were blank, all waiting to be carved. All dreamed.

Then the gate opened and I was led through the court, through the glowing opened portal, through the dimmed hall, its vast walls hung with fringes.

On the way to the first chamber, dark, polished teakwood shone, as if in the falling rainwater. Those who looked wonderingly at it and saw an otter were not admitted.

On the way to the second chamber, the lighter and the darker woods mottled each other, braided with interlace. No one who cried out as if at an adder was permitted to pass.

On the way to the third chamber, the walls were leathern and darkened gold. Those who fancied that the smell of earth was there were all turned away.

On the way to the fourth chamber, strange pictures hung: a glass of green fur, an open apple, a house of loss; and portraits of the Baron of Grass, the Count of Nought. Those who approached to read the titles had to go all the way back.

On the way to the fifth chamber, all was smooth and slate, as if beauty were a disease of surface, an encroachment of depth. Many fell asleep, and had to be removed.

On the way to the sixth chamber, everything was mirrored, yea even to mirroring itself. Those who felt within them even the faintest twitch of answering light were struck blind.

On the way to the seventh chamber, the amethyst and sapphire
   light ceased and there were glimmering marble slabs. They
   dazzled mine eyes, and it was not at my own tears that I
   cried out *O water! Water!* Thus I was never to enter.

RED

Along the wide canal
Vehement, high flashings
Of sunlight reflect up
From rock, from bunker, from
Metal plate. In the mild
Shade of his waiting place—
Shade a gourd might afford—
J sits embracing his
Automatic weapon,
Crowned by a sloppy cap,
Inhaling the fire of
White air from the parched east.

J is exceedingly
Glad of the gourd—of his
Arp-shaped drop of shadow,
Its eye-shaped stain—but the
Flashings have prepared a
Worm of white fire, blazing
With an unseen pain the
Whites of his eyes to blank.
Red winds lash his throat, then
Blood bubbles into milk,
Shit and pale viscera
Drop into soured honey.

Into the morning fire,
Into the white fighting,

Tender olive bird plucked
Out of Leviathan,
Out of a statehood, grim
And necessary, he
Has hung through the unjust
Noon, fire at his right hand,
The fierce ghost of his sire;
At his left, waiting to
Stain its flames to crimson,
Dark of his bloody dam.

For forty winks in the
Desert, his eyelids clank
Down. Then, the fiery worm:
Unwilling prophet of
His past, he sees screaming
Seals ripped open, vision
Uncurling, as can by
Opened can the film of
The ages runs in coils
Across his mind's sky: Bronze
Spears smash grayware pitchers,
Torches splash fear near tents;

Slow, greaved legs clang along
Parasangs of gray road;
Brave and fair embrace the
Bad and dark; arrows snap
Against square parapets;
Sons of the desert rise;
Gray, wreathed heads lock crowns on
Blond curls; the bright tower
Is truly taken; there
Are kingdoms, there are songs
Along the wall————but his
Films melt into jelly:

Now at his red moment
He forgets his city
As his tongue is made to
Fuck the roof of his mouth,
His skull cradling little
Ones of brain is dashed now
Against rock, and the pulp
Of him slips to the ground.
Blood, rooted in earth, makes
Adam's kingdom, Adom,
Fruit brought forth of iron,
The wide realm of the red.

Ox, door, water—these huge simples of our life become red in the grounding sun, stained with the same red. Through the door we see the ox awaiting water. Our pottery is red with black figures of valor. Our ploughshares are honed for tomorrow; by the door, the wooden yoke is grim with nails.

Here at our crimson heroic, the painter images us by dipping into his pot of primaries; the singer keeps returning to *a*.

But we know the color of our bordering flame to arise from the warm deepening of yellow, from the cold intensifying of azure. The darkened line of sun and sky is our rim of blood.

Thus we are always at our westernmost here. If our light goes out, let the rest of you beware.

By night, a red one meanders among the starfields, gathering eyefulls of light: not the Warrior, but the bloodied Saturn, suffused with lateness.

By day, the iron sickle leans against the wall; ringing around a pot, its blade reddens with rust.

By twilight in the courtyard, a pool of water lies quietly cupped in a block of dented stone; in its red mirror the sky, the turreted wall and a peering, eyeing head all are reddened, as in the ambient light of the Last Day.

The red singer sits looking back toward the violet becoming black. His songs are capable of the opened and the spilled; only for them the wind sings in his hair. He stands outside the door: his shadow falls across it. Blown dust makes a false threshold.

ORANGE

The age of awakening: bright
With drops from the crushed, segmented
Sun, the rising hemisphere of
Huge Florida orange. As the
Jupiter Home Juice Extractor
Recoils from its pressures, the dross
Of pulp and rind remain, and the
Innocent air of unhurried
Cold morning widens. But not with
Promises: for nothing adverse
Has ever occurred; promises
That it is never to happen
Need not yet have been invented.
The ear of air is widened by
The sounds of so very many
Individual energies!
They are hoarding light as from the
Traffic of their exaltation
Arises the tone of bright horns
Filling air and aureate ear
With hearsay of the threshing-out
Of gain. Windows facing eastward

Burn with a pale orange fire, as
If loss were being flamed away.

Drops of orange juice that Midas
Thirsts for are turned into burning
Bullets; later on he will be
Trapped inside a cunt of metal,
Pinched for his silly pains by the
Hard parody of flesh into
Which the soft parts of a person
Freeze at his caress. But what of
The God's touch in the Age of Cold?
—Frail Danaë, guarded only
By brazen contrivances, lies
Back, open to the god of gold
Who comes like coins thumbed into her
Slot: squish, chunk. He spends; they melt in
Her; the god has got his hero,
The daughter of brass alloyed, her
Mortality bought, with massy
Gold. Not with the juice of sunlight
Streaming with magnificence does
The crude chrysomorph enter her,
But like light interred in the hard
Shining that dazzles poor eyes with
Mere models of the immortal.

But these fables from the fountain
Of the age of orange themselves
Harden, and the grayer stages
Of the day we create by our
Separations—the juice from the
Crushed vessel of shell, the refined
Metal from the crusty rock—are
Even at best the residues
Of arising. When we heed the

Silly fictions—choosing the lead
Above the gold, the chevelure
Over the brocade—we make our
Moral from the living dullard
Of daylight, not the gleaming dead
God. Here in the gloaming of the
Ages of His Images, we
Pluck the orange flower, or press
The arrant philtre and with a
Midas touch of tongue proclaim an
Oral gold, like Circe turning
Everything of worth into the
Travesty of value, and like
The god putting off the golden,
Squeezing out of it the gold.

"Orange dies out in the ascending fire," roared our grayish remainder; "Gold is a dream of lead," said Roy G. Biv.

When gold can be alloyed to form a working metal, then the Order of Ages will be changed. "But only when it is as common as copper," retorted the stupid jewel of the floor; "Only when it is as dull as lead," said Roy G. Biv.

"Gold is gold," say the sages. "Lead is lead," say the thieves. "What's lead is gold and what's gold is lead," says Roy G. Biv.

All the colors are fractions of white. All the colors burn up in the unseen higher vibrations of glory. "But when I muddied them all in a sty of pigments, when I put them all in the dish and mixed and mixed, all I got was the leaden tone of earth," said Roy G. Biv.

The gleaming of their ruined gold outlasts the kingdoms. "But the mud and the rock around it will prevail," insists the lustreless plumber; "Hurrah for the dull," says Roy G. Biv.

After the gold, the dross; after the juice, the cracked shell; after the emptying, the hollow. "Ah, yes," sighed Rex Cloacarum; "That's me," said Roy G. Biv.

The painter said: "If one were to imagine a bluish orange, it would have to feel like a southwesterly north wind." "No, that would be a reddish green," said the other painter. "It is all the same to me," said Roy G. Biv.

Blessed art thou who bringest forth fruit of the bronze: bells and pomegranates, thunder and lightning. Blessed are thou who brought forth nought of the lead, save Roy G. Biv.

YELLOW

Dirty gold sublimed from the black earth up
In bright air: these are the awaited stalks,
The ripeness possible to imagine
Even among mezzotints of winter,
And to remember having imagined
Oddly amid late spring's lackadaisies
And all of the earlier primulas.
Prophetic pale flecks of forsythia
Lemony against the cold engravings
Of gray branches—these whisper of golden
Flashings over the surface of water
Above the attentive images of
Jonquils peering out at themselves along
The wide bank. Which would be no fulfillment
In any event, of early pallor:
It would remain an interpretation
Of the flimsy text, half unremembered,
Dimming evermore and diminishing.

Like gold afire in the yellow candles'
Flame, steady with remembrances and now
And then only wavering in regret,
What might have been burns up and the bright fruit
Of what we after all have ever ripens.
The squinting flames eye each other as fruit
And flame and eye and yellowy flower.
To have been kept, to have reached this season,
Is to have eternized, for a moment,
The time when promise and fulfillment feed
Upon each other, when the living gold
Of sunlight struck from the amazing corn
Seems one with its cold, unending token,
The warm time when both seem reflections from
The bright eyes of the Queen of the Peaceful
Day being welcomed with these twin burnings,
These prophetic seeds of the Ripener,
Brightness rising and getting on with things.

Or: In the air there is a soft gleaming
As of fair light in certain hair, and wind
Through the pale curtains streaming like moonlight
In the dark air that fills all the rooms of
Dreaming like a perfumed tune that will ne'er . . .
(Vanish? A snuffed lamp in the dream of day?)
This has been all of silver. But see now:
The man of earth exhales a girl of air,
Of her light who lies beside him, gentle
And bare, under the living shawl of all
Her long hair, while her short below softly
Touches his tired thigh with welcoming.
It is that she is there. It is the pure
Return of everlastingness in her
Hands and the readiness of the sweet pear
In the touch of her mouth that fill the air
—Even the air within the circle of

His emptied arms—with light beyond seeming.

The possible metal underwater,
Beer-can or amulet, its reflections
More important than those of the surface
(Remember those jonquils we had before),
This is one thing: but another matter
Is of the precious glare in eloquent
Watery surfaces—in them, but not
Of them. And all that matters in the end
Is of the moment of late, fine morning
When the world's yellow is of burning sands
Leading down to the penultimate blue
Of, say, the Ionian Sea whose waves
Gave light that had to have been of their own
And which, when darkened momently by the
Cool shadows of our gaze, plucked up the deep
Hues of our gleaming feet at the bottom
Of our golden bodies in their purest
And most revealing element at last.

All the eternal ornaments set down in dust will never live nor yet give birth. Pale, unenduring petals go to brown and therefore live in the soft mines of earth. EPHRAIM DU BLÉ ENGRENIER

The leaves ripen for the harvest wind, yellow and red. But it is the trees he threshes; it is their branches that will be stored.

The dark lines of goldenness afire, shifted leftward by too much hastening away from us, reside in a region more of the red than of the yellow we have delighted in.

Of which an anecdote: We had backed further and further up the steps as the splendors before us continued. Gleaming processions passed this way and that: distantly, along the great Causeway of white marble, and further away, spiralling slowly to the top of the southern mountain, and nearby, back and forth across the columned bridges, along the ramparts rising above the shining bay. None seemed headed in the same direction. The crowds watching, like the one in which we found ourselves, seemed like the passing throngs—in white, in gold, in armor or in many-colored silks—to be filling the wide air, in a full celebration that could not quite be called gratitude. We backed further on up the steps below a statue that rose behind us, perhaps their famous chryselephantine Saturn, golden-scythed. The high sun was far from its reddened setting. But it would only be after that lowering crimson, rhymed in the red fires of the Conquerors come that same evening that, as we fled past the base of the statue, past the stone pedestal on which it rested, we should discern it indeed to have been one of Mars, sword curved in the same flat crescent as scythe, gatherer of red rather than of yellow.

Hilda laid on the gold leaf. The copy she was making of "The Miracle of the Field" flourished and sprouted under her shining care. It was not that it was a copy, nor that it was not even after some lost original. It was that it was hers. This was true plenty.

GREEN

The swallows and the early crickets with a blurred
Squeak scratched at the clear glass of the coming evening.
It was not yet dark: the surrounding green was still
Green, as if day had intended to leave a trace
Of something other than deadened gray in the black
That was to be, unmindful of the night's utter
Incapability of making remainders

Of the green into something of its own, some hushed
Nocturnal verdant. But the birds and the bugs sang
Not of this, nor of hope deepened into appalled
Silence: they chanted of nothing that was to be,
Of nothing. In the unlost green they chanted on.

In the high day, clear at the viridian noon,
Blue water, enisled in the broad grass singing hot
Choruses of summer, lies still; and far away
Half-gesturing lakes surrounded by dense, quiet
Spruces recall the silence that we are told lies
As a green hedge around blue wisdom. At the edge
Of things here and now, soft-looking cedars, waving
Away at azure, keep the sky at a distance.
If there is a leak in this green, it will have run
Into the pool, given it something of itself,
Which, rinsed in the shrillest glare of sun in water,
Will prove blue, blue derived from the wide green beyond.

And then, as if echoing all the other tones,
The noises of green thickened, and the quivering
Ground heaved gently back where it was trod upon
As if presence upon it were an entering,
Not to subvert the soft grass whose high coloring
Was that of the far heart that lay deep below them.
The tuned muscles of the earth gripped the roots around,
And yielded up unheard joy, a sobbing of mud;
Above there was a laughter of grass in delight
At the sunny loving two bright bodies contrived,
Stained with pale green, bruising the yet uncooled lawn,
    watched
Only by their own uninterested shadows.

Nomad among the verdures, you watch dark actions
Before the arras of firs, the passionless spread
Of algae only whose element throbs; pausing

In your wide amble among the phenomena
You drink the shade of the plane, and remember the
Other places of pausing, the pleasances of
Tone. Wanderer, flinging off the gauzes of day,
You too will awaken from the dust of eyesight
To the polar, the total, awaiting all with
The patience of the deep that black has when green ends,
The still unquenchable absorption of its gaze.
It will not be, can never be a mere return.

Man will nicht weiter, und man kann nicht weiter: we
Desire nothing beyond this being of green
Nor can we reach it; and even that overworked
Part of us, the eye, wearied of the vivid, stuffed
With the beneficence of leaf, seeks not to raise
Itself toward the new giddiness of heaven, clear
Though that blue may be—it would be to leave too much
Behind, the old heaviness of earth—but vaulting
The whole sequence of empurplings to alight in
Blackness, if anywhere else, in the condensed dust
Of being seen as green, turning to which darkness
Is no roving of vision, no dimming of trust.

Green: no flag of what state one is in—no peaceful
Islam widening in its cool exhalations;
No region of unreadiness; no pallor of
Young ghosts, hungry but with unbudded taste, not yet
Dyed into ripe life; no chill at body's absence;
No calmly open emblem of onward, no Go.
Stop, Traveller, here at the center of lamplight.
See how these green meanings reach even into
Unenvying meadows of mown grain, even through
Eyelike encircling blue: the green alone, unmown
As its ranked exemplars are not, buzzes with what
Is, breathes with ever-presence, with its verity.

We who have come to this work too late, our time long past the age of missions, our own years and days turned on the road downward—we will tell ourselves, if we fail, that we were not too late, but too soon.

Instructions from the engineers to Werth: the Ponte Milvio, despite the rebuilding, may need bracing. A salvage barge would perhaps be better than working off the bridge itself; and inaccuracies in estimating the weight of the Lamp must be allowed for. But the rig suggested in the enclosed plans will probably work. Gelb is quite convinced of this, and the raising of the Lamp is, after all, his part of the project.

Krasny arrived late last night, from the far west. We met as scheduled by the dank republican temples, by a forest of tram-lines; dirty, excavated only fifty years ago, somewhat overgrown, this place has never been pictorialized. Now it is awash with cats, dark below the red sunset.

Aside from the unutterable difficulty of the task itself—translating the Lamp, an Object which is somehow like a Text, across national boundaries as across a tract of time—there is the problem of all the replicas. Sagol is still not sure that all of them have been located. Sources like *Der begrabene Leuchter* (1937) are, alas, not to be trusted. Sagol is now convinced that there is something hidden in one of the old forts of the Morea; in the Peloponnesus. This will occasion a difficult overland journey if we are all to stay together. We had hoped to leave Venice by water.

One should have thought that there would be twelve of us. Two to mislead, of course; they would assist in no way with the recovery of the Lamp, but would merely fill out vacant spaces in a paradigm, would seem to be two more of us when, in fact, they would not be of *us* at all. Pomaranczowy laughed when I proposed this: "Two more to pay, two more sets of petty cash vouchers, and for nothing at all?" No, it would have been for something. The others? If there were really only ten, then, three would have had to remain unknown to the rest. Can that actually be the case now? I believe—we all believe—that we are seven. Kuan, our pilot, arrives tomorrow.

Gelb has found an old guidebook of Rome—by one Octavian Blewitt, 1850—with the well-known passage (about the Lamp having fallen into the Tiber at the same moment that the body of Maxentius was thrown off the bridge) marked in fading ink. There is a page of scrawl interleaved; I shall translate it later when there will be time.

To "find"—how peculiar a verb, so guarded in its perfective aspect. It cannot be used progressively except figuratively, with the *but . . . but . . .* of wit. Thus: "Buy this for me!" "Be patient, I am buying it"—well enough; but "Find it!" "I *am* finding it"—no he is not; his use of "find" here lies somewhere between figure of speech and that mode of lying, unmarked by the rhetoricians, of the whole for the part. Yet "find" is unrelated, after all, to "final," to endings. Its cousins are Latin bridges, Greek sea, and our own "path"; it emerged from an earlier life of sense in "to come upon." Some day when we think of these times will grammar permit us to say "We were gradually coming upon the Lamp" but not "We were finding it"?

How we are to get it out of Rome is only part of the problem, though; it has to be carried across to its home in the un-imaged region, bare of representations save those of itself. Actual smaller copies of the Lamp, brass or bronze doodads as *objets de virtù* or adapted for use on minor occasions of commemoration have been expressly forbidden for centuries. Perhaps it was thus that so many images of it sprang up. The

linear version of it cut in the stone at Sardis is flanked by its
tender echo in nature—a frond? a leaf? a ramified trunk?
Whichever, its central shaft is flanked by five linear arms on
each side. A tree of eleven branches? What can it mean? Is
one point missing? Is one to be disregarded? Or is it merely
the inability of nature truly to signify beyond any one moment?

Questing: When there is only one task left, it is in great danger
of becoming merely the image of a task. After all the great
quests were done, there was the questing after new quests;
but that lay outside the series and was not a part of it. We
lie among the ruins of questing, here at noon on the Palatine.
The grass, the sharp acanthus, the cypresses and dark umbrella
pines: they guard and possess these broken stones. What kind
of questing could proceed among these degrees of green? If
we were embarked on a quest for the Lamp, we should surely
fail: but the finding has been done. We must raise it, carry
it, destroy the replicas and make restitution in the place of loss.

At the exact point of noon—at just noon—the sundial's vertical
finger will be a knife edge, almost invisible. But even without
the dial, we will know the moment from the grass: it will be
at its greenest, remembering its early dimness when it awoke
to light, invisibly dreaming its darkness to come. These are
what saturate its hue, giving it depth and strength now, now.

A strangely-cut, seven-faceted stone, darker than any emerald
I have seen. Werth threw it down upon the table today; it
must have weighed 200 carats or more. Each of the facets, like
an odd-shaped eye, surveyed us, the room, the maps, the salvage equipment. The *carabinieri* uniforms hung on a rack in
the corner; the enamel paint and spraying apparatus were
piled up across from them. It was as if the minimal but precise
technology which had faceted the stone, had given it windows
onto the world of those who watched it, stood as a kind of

rebuke to our sleazy gadgetry. But what else is there to use?
The nations of the earth pray to their gods with the same
words and means of connecting them that are employed in
telling white lies, in complaining that they have been cheated
by the butcher. Our nouns are chains and hydraulic lifts, the
underwater gear our tropes.

Kuan, the airman, has a theory that when the Lamp has been
restored, the famous image of it here will vanish. That large,
noble stone relief from oblivion—the only representation we
have all had to go on—is by its very nature uncanonical. It is
as if one lived by a Scripture whose original tongue had been
totally forgotten, all other texts in it lost or defaced, and that
had only been preserved in a mocking and contemptuous translation, elegantly but insincerely done. And yet it would have
had to have done for one's Text. When I ask Kuan if the
surrounding stone lictors on the relief, if Vespasian, Titus, and
Domitian will vanish too, he snorts: "Those that were imaged
have gone: stone may remain. When the Lamp is restored, the
frail, impermanent representation will immediately wear away.
All stone is as the grass, gray grass." I joke in my way, Kuan
in his.

If the restoration is successful, we shall all hear of it as if a
general roar had gone up in the atmosphere. If it fails, or if,
the mission having been accomplished, the time is not yet
ready to absorb its consequences, we shall hear nothing. Our
lives will all go on as before. But the transporting will, if
having been done, have been done for all time.

These are the replicas: (1) At Ferrara; the bronze one—a poor
copy with no base—has been unearthed and is on its way here.
It will be substituted for the Lamp and given over to the
Belle Arti people as what we had dredged up, so that no
Antiquity will be, as far as they know, leaving Italy. The
historians were right about this one; Beatrice de Luna, living

in the Veneto in the late 1540s, had it made and hidden there before she left for Constantinople. *"La Señora"*—what a legacy we have from her! (2) At Cordoba, outside the walls; this was destroyed in the attack there in July, 1936. (3) In Alexandria, lost overboard at sea when the lashings of its crate broke in a storm, 1956. (4) At Antioch, dating from the fourth century; this is to be blown up in an internecine terrorist attack. (5) And now, it appears, this last one at Karytaina. This will be my task; the others will avoid the Greek mainland after all. I shall proceed from Patras.

The interleaved notes from the old Roman guidebook: "The Pictorial Land . . . Hilda said [illegible] . . . was a meaning and purpose in each of its seven branches, and such a [illegible] cannot be lost forever. When it is found . . . as each branch [illegible] a differently colored lustre from the other six . . . shall combine into the intense white light of truth." This is all I can make out. O, the musings of tourists, moving among the ruins and the replicas!

That we should have to carry it back Eastward seems to confirm our task as one of restitution. The labors of Hercules all moved progressively Westward. There are no more heroes of the sun; ours is one labor gathered from the work of many. Just as colored lights can stain each other's field of radiance, so an imperfection in the work of any of us could impair the validity of the work of any of the others.

The great narratives are of finding and of founding. What was hidden in our case had already been found, what was to be established has been long since. Our romance is of raising and bearing, the undoing of histories. Consider: a victorious sign flew into the sky for Constantine—the antithetical Lamp to be buried tumbled off the bridge into the Tiber. It had been kept for 237 years in Vespasian's Temple of Peace. We still do not know why it was removed or by whom, on the day of Constantine's victory. In December we shall dredge it up and take it back. This is almost a comic enterprise; and save for our skills, we are the usual comically ill-assorted lot: Krasny for security, Pomaranczowy, our paymaster and bursar, Gelb, the engineer, Werth, at the center of things, Kuan, our pilot, myself, and Sagol who navigates, plots and times. We resemble a collection of types sent up from central casting, and rejected even by Cinecittà because we looked too obvious. Perhaps in the cold light of a winter dawn, our truck snorting up the Lungotevere Flaminio, we shall look less so. But it will not matter.

Werth says that the replica in Greece is the most important one of all, the most perfect, the most false. It was in all probability the one carried to Constantinople by Belisarius. The Vandals removed many treasures from Rome to Carthage in 455. It was probably there and then that replica was made; Justinian received it as genuine in the Eastern capital and there it remained. Procopius's fiction that it was sent back, with other valuables, to Jerusalem lest they prove unlucky for the Emperor is to be totally discounted. And so it remained in Byzantium. But for how long? I shall be spending the summer and autumn designing the removal; perhaps I can determine the history as well, even as I plan to end it.

That I am a kind of afterthought, a substitute on this mission, doesn't bother me; that I may fail does. That I am not to participate in the raising of the Lamp from the mud doesn't; that by some mishap I may not be there to help carry it in and over does. But it seems that wanting what is reasonable to want is itself hopeless, unreasonable and wasteful. All I have ever deserved is to be able to work at this. I shall not say "serve"—that is the language of all those nasty royal arms which proclaim indifferently *"Non Serviam"* or *"Ich Dien"*. Blazon liars. What we do is beyond serving.

At the beginning I would sit among the ruins and gaze like any pictorialist on what had been lost, and what saved—the tender sculpture of chance leaves three columns, an artfully broken piece of pediment, standing at the sentimental height midway between the composed and the sublime. I would gaze at the ruins and contemplate not reconstruction, not restoration, but restitution. What we were planning, what was being planned for us, was a serious trifling with history. Brooding over the ruins summoned up regrets: if only the barbarians' powder had been wet; if the fire had burned the other way; if the Emperor's sad, wise cousin had seized the purple . . . if, if. But this is like contemplating the ruins of one's own years. One comes to hate what was lost, but to admire the tumbled drums of column lying at provocative angles against other stones, to despise the once-finished and gleaming structure, and still to hum to oneself, droningly and incessantly, "if . . . if."

The raising itself: the date set for Sunday, November 30, at an early hour. An accident on the bridge will provide an excuse for a work crew. I shall have left the previous night, not getting to see the Lamp until we all meet again, content with a last glimpse of Werth's gleaming green stone, not standing for the thing itself, but speaking wordlessly of it. It shows a hard, cold radiance that shines outwardly through all of its ocular facets because of the excited reflections and bendings of its inner light. And thus, like all significant shapes, a picture of the attention that regards that shape as well—as what lies behind the eye perceives itself in the depths and surfaces of the smallest spill of water on a black tabletop, or in the profoundest pool set in a cup of mountain. And thus, like these, the stone is a minor text but a canonical one. It will be like, that night, a verse to speed the departure of The Last Day Before—"The earth has given its yield: may we be blessed. . . ." (A yield of green? Of stone? Of light?) I shall be driving through the dark chilling night to the south.

Karytaina. It was one of the twelve major baronies under Geoffrey de Villehardouin whose own castle lay to the south in Kalamata. The Frankish fort was built by Sir Hugh de Bruyères in 1254, sold to Andronikes II Palaiologos in 1320, taken by the Turks ca. 1460. The fort crowns the flat, rocky brow of the high town like a dull coronet, heavy and important. The replica lies under the stones of the parapet that faces southeast. The University archeological dig will have loosened the principal one, and the simplest and most silent of equipment will unearth the replica. If it cannot be destroyed on the spot, melted down right away, the helicopter will take it out with me. There is no great problem here, as the sole charge is to remove the replica from future history, soundlessly, unnoticed and without any consequences save for those that stem from the recovery of the Lamp itself.

If it were only that my parents had been poor, but had not quarreled always: it would have served. If they had battled continually, but had not used me as a broom handle: it would have served. If they had used me to brandish and bang only, but had not gone on to explain why this had to be: it would have been enough. If they had explained and expounded only, but not sent me away: it would have been enough. If they had sent me away only, but it had not been to a Home: it would have served. If I had only been sent to a Home, but had not become a model inmate: plenty. If I had become a model inmate, but the Home had not thereupon burned to the ground: it would have served. If the Home had been destroyed, but I had not in addition injured my left foot: it would have been enough. If I had only remained forever halt, but had not made a bad bargain with the crutchmaker: it would have served. If my crutch were inadequate, but I had not quested after another sort of succedaneum and prop to my infirmities: it would have been enough. If I had womanized my way into near madness only, and had not found a suitable and treacherous helpmeet: it would have sufficed. If my wife had but dug away at the Temple of My Heart only and had not taken years and years to do so: it would have sufficed. If years of hopeful peace had made the crash deafening, but I had at least been able to move from the spot: *basta!* BUT, since I could not walk away from my disasters, being stunned and rocked with grief, I saw the shadow of one stone falling across another as the day slowly breathed; I felt a nearness; I saw the task of the slowness itself of tasks. It all served. I am prepared now even for joy.

La Señora: Doña Gracia Nasi as she reconstituted herself, shedding the blessing of moonlight, journeying in the commerce of restitution from Lisbon to Amsterdam to Venice and finally to Constantinople. Perhaps it was then, at the time when her nephew and son-in-law was Duke of Naxos, that the replica was removed westward. It travelled from island to island hidden among manifest cargoes; the sailings of the summer days brought its hidden gold to Nauplion. By weeks of overland journey to the river, south of Megalopolis; by barge down the Alpheus to Karytaina, its tall head of mountain waiting at the dark high end of the long Arcadian valley. The Duke of Naxos, at the crest of his fortunes, accomplishes the queen of his acts. Why? In the knowledge that it was indeed a replica? This makes little sense. But in the prophetic modernity of not knowing, and of not daring to decree or predict? Perhaps.

I feel strangely young, as if I had acquired new qualities: the power to charm, a speaking and cheerful gaze, an aura of fragility that was somehow nonetheless being protected, and thus remaining uncoarsened by any defenses of its own. I am to embark not on a night journey, but upon a pastoral cycle of magic and simplifications. I can almost read the touchingly conventional phases of my tale. *Book I:* He drives through the night and the next day rests in Bari. *Book II:* The episode of the lady in the hotel at Brindisi. *Book III:* Terrorists attack the ferry and take the lady hostage, but dare not return to the Albanian coast. *Book IV:* The Lady escapes on Corfù; the others in Rome are notified. *Book V:* The ferry limps on to Patras; he discovers her letter. *Book VI:* Meanwhile—all has gone well in Rome; the Lamp is on its way northward. *Book VII:* Alarms in Patras; escape down the coast to Pyrgos; return north again. *Book VIII:* The lady and the producer's yacht. *Book IX:* He and she meet again on Zante. *Book X:* *"Zante, fior' di Levante";* the Old Man of the Island. *Book XI:* The vineyards of currants; narrative of the Old Man of Zante. *Book XII:* Meanwhile—the ship *Teva* out of Nicosia has sailed from Chioggia; the Lamp is on the water. *Book XIII:* The sad departure from Zante; they separate on the mainland; he meets his driver. *Book XIV:* The terrorists again: we have not seen the last of them; a narrow escape in Kyparissia. *Book XV:* Meanwhile—*Teva* in the Ionian Sea; the lady imprisoned by Customs. *Book XVI:* On the road; along the river; among the mountains; a digression on Mount Lykaion. *Book XVII:* He reaches Karytaina and confers with the archeologists; songs of the Sweet Singer of Karytaina. *Book XVIII:* Meanwhile—*Teva* off Cyprus; a storm at sea; the Lamp nearly lost overboard. *Book XIX:* Night in Karytaina; a veiled visitor at the inn: it is the lady; she reveals herself to be Fräulein Werth, the sister of our coördinator. *Book XX:* The replica; carrying it down into the valley: it is impossible to melt down; awaiting the helicopter. *Book XXI:* No news from the ship; resourcefulness of Fräulein Werth; the helicopter. *Book XXII:* The replica dropped into the sea; meanwhile—the Lamp is put safely ashore in darkness. *Book XXIII:* He and she. . . . But the last book-and-a-half of every story is always incomplete by virtue of its very closure: to finish is to leave undone the task of showing eternity, rushing out of the last event in a stream of consequences, mostly lost, like bubbles near a source. But the stream itself is all there will ever be. Now from the north the *tramontana* has come up; it blows through my pages. The umbrella pines have darkened, with evening, into the color of painted foliage under old varnish. I close the covers of my pastoral romance, dark, nubbly, green leather printed in gold, the color of the dissolving trees.

It will not go this well. Or this badly.

The Lamp has been subject only to time.

But we are now thrust into the midst of things. The summer afternoon, *romancier,* dies not with the light of the sun, but with the radiance of its own green. I think now, with the days of autumn waiting before me, of the impending grays and browns. The time of waiting is the time of rock. And my vision must narrow to the task.

I can see my moment now. Not the time of accomplishment—that instant is ever invisible, dissolved in the eddies of occurrence. I can look into the heart of the eternal first seconds of the view—from a point southeast along that Arcadian valley—of the mountain village. The sun rakes across it before sinking down behind Mount Lykaion, to the southwest; the neck of the hill embraced by the houses, the brow garlanded by the crenellated stones, the usual layers of fortification blend into the pictorial dusk: Frankish, Byzantine, Turkish. The Venetians did not touch here. My lamed eye reaches down the valley toward its dark head, whose own blind gaze commands the view toward the plain behind me. The far space and long antiquity give meaning to each other, the relation of mineral hill and ethereal sky being an encounter of very ancient presences. And yet this is an occasional vision, a wandering of the eye among accidents. It is not, say, of the long-proposed Ascent of something, planned, undertaken with a companion, glossed by a text, warned against by the rustic on the slopes, moralized on the way up and the way down, impelled in the first place by the reductively described desire to see the height—to see from, of, and toward the height—of what had always been, from the surrounding countryside of one's life, ever in view. It is not even the view toward the Pisgah from which the hedged promise of the to-be-arrived-at will gleam, to, but not for, the climber in the sunset. It is not the binocular seizure of detail, nor the important zoom into what matters for the task at hand. It is not of reaching height; it is not of squat failure. It is of the surroundingness.

BLUE

I

Day is naked even in its nuances
Of cloud: and there goes Pancho Manza, *homme*
De terre, working his own way alongside
The wide road that bandages the rye fields.

Moving along the grain, a point of shade,
He will arrive in good time to keep his
Disappointment with the dim, elusive
Horizon: stumpety-stump. Across the

Road, nightly the dark don, Freiherr of Sky,
Waits by a small pool, floating bright sequins
Over velvety water: one after
Another, they mirror diminutions

Of moon, upon which the pondering don
Reflects, his eyes lit windows of the room
Wherein crafty lamplight is at its work
On objects, and silence settles its dust.

2

At the broad border of the evening
Mercury leered out of the bold cobalt
He was returning to, remembering
Azure anterior to this night's share.

He remembered cyan: he thought again
Of high, blue air he had borne a white torch
Of morning in, of what it was to hear
The blue zones of sky torn with humming winds.

His tiny globe glowed brightly with knowing
How to tell blue from blue, where noon divides
The after from the forenight. Later, when
He knelt down among deep, waving shadows,

He smelled the exploding smalt of the sea
Fizzing away in a different kind
Of light: its hue cried out against fancy,
Against tales of its own contingency

(Such as that once a blue moon setting dipped
Deep in the broad water, dyeing it).
Above it the undying barer of
Fresh, borrowed light stared out of the blue dawn.

3

Better to say perhaps that there were two
Moons, one blue and one yellow, that green tones
Were but diseases of these, or the fruit
Of their contention at times of twilight;

And that the major illusion of moon
Was one of widening at the zenith—

Not at the seedy horizon behind
Cutout low rooftops, or second-growth woods,

The better to condense their silhouettes—
And that the creamy moonlight, spilled among
Our forms of night, fled the neutrality
Of silver kissing marble shapes in myths,

Likewise the icy light of the witch's
Eye, which drew away from like tinsellings.
Then nothing would affright the traveller
Of thicket paths: neither the yellow-made

Shade cast behind him, the Body of Bones,
Nor the blue-flung shadow of the Body
Of Work moving more slowly before him.
He would be calmed by the two modes of night.

4

But a sole moon alone hovers above
The fields of collapsed light, the acreage
Of our misfortunes, narrowed at its height;
And the hard blue line of the horizon

Divides two notional hues of ocean
Cloudy with whitecaps and of sky behind
The day's mackerel belly; it slices
Our globe of eyesight, and bluer than might

Be imagined, far more lethal than all
The bottled light of fluorescent tubes,
Unleashes the strong eager energies
Of destruction, new shatterings under

The sun, new nullifications at night.
Dawn comes when we distinguish blue from—white?
No, green—and, in agreement, eyeing the
Dying dark, our morning wariness nods.

You had best build one yourself; when bought already assembled, these things work very badly, and may leave dangerous residues.

The laser-eye is itself dangerous, for like a speaking, destroying word of light it can nullify your subjects as if they were
chaoses, but leave you not alone, merely a hologram of yourself and yet accompanied still.

The control panel is located deep inside, although an unre-
liable terminal is available at the top, from which there is a
synoptic but distorted view of the power units.

Do not make the mistake of sentimentalizing the mechanical
parts: for the flywheel, archaic and precise with its gleaming
spokes, is a horror of solemnity, going berserk at the insinua-
tions of jiggle—the twin moons of the governor are a cramp
on exuberance—the pistons slide easily joylessly in their cold
oil—the valves twist with difficulty—the shining brass gauges
were unwisely calibrated in a time of hope.

The mercury is another matter: its drops cohere so—oily but
dry, like seeds of gleaming—cold sparks hinting of the tiny
hot planet. It will get out of hand; yet it is absolutely essential
to the working.

There can be great variation in the exterior design; one has
seen many playful arrangements—some resemble machines to
make or to break. But it is the circuits alone which are terrify-
ing, and the interior spaces whose tolerances are so minute.

The energy it consumes is enormous; it is almost too expensive to operate. But of course, one must.

Those to be dealt with need not be specially prepared.

After the red alert light goes off, there will be a period of waiting; do not disintegrate them at this stage, or you too will never have existed.

Wait for the blue light to shine.

Remember that they are all despots.

If you get it to work properly, it will put an end to them, your predecessors.

DEPARTED INDIGO

My father as a boy knew her
As a gracious, kind and hooded
Lady, and her house at forty
Four hundred something Ängstrom Street
(One never needed the numbers:
It was near the end of the road)
Was open. By my day her place
Of residence was gone, its lot
Obscured by neighboring mansions.

When she dwelt among us her deep
Gaze comforted beyond smiling.
The fragile virgin of Justice
Frowned at the way things were to be
And fled, but our lost lady would
Never reign at arms' length: she loved

Her subject surfaces, but not
Those alone: a secret consort
Drank of her darkness, she of his.

Was she Madame de Violet
Or good Frau Blau? We were not told.
But where she lay she joined all hands
About her—not like the heated
Gold mediations of Venus,
Fanning the leftward yellow flames
Of her limping smith, while sharing
In the abashed reddening of
Her netted warrior rightward—

Our far lady lay among her
Saturations on either side,
Reflecting an intensity
That both possessed—the blue of day
Sky, and the violet of night—
Filling the glass pitchers of their
Transparency with a common
Pool of dark dew, from which they drank
And which suffused them with themselves.

It was for the other side of
Sunset that we needed her dark,
Connecting tone, for the richness
Of aftermath, to represent
It even to ourselves. Some said
It was so that blue be followed
By something of blue, violet
Be preceded by something of
Violet, lest they both die out;

Others felt that her realm lay just
Beyond sufficiency, making

Unacknowledged legislations
Of the rainbow, crowding her zone
Among the belts of the body
Of light: they knew this to be the
Last part of the necessary.
(What is enough? There is only
Too much, or now, in the twilight

Of abandonment, too little)
But later commentators, born
Under our poor hexarchy of
Tone may wonder how defenders
Of design can have known of her
Superfluity of hue when
It still lay among the chambers
Of color, as one of the great
Hours of Day occupies his throne.

Now, in the regions of vision
Where she dwells—not like that first frail
Maiden who fled into starlight,
A mere novel constellation,
But between these touching points of
Light—the rich, hopeful darkness seems
Deepened by her presence, under
Which we live and, hushed, still breathe the
Night air's perfume of discernment.

There are six songs, no, seven, that need to be sung in the darkness:

The Battle on the Plains, where heroes stood and fell; the Finding of the Treasure where it was hard to get to; the Founding of the Fields, where all expanded in peace; the

Dancing on the Lawns where there was nothing wrong; the Visit to the Sky, which was no wearying journey; the Farewell to the Guide, when the next stage was reached; the Darkening of It All, when it had become too late.

At first our heroes stood for us, then among us, when we stood for ourselves; now they do not even represent our sorrows. The Paul Bunyan balloon was deflated and put away when Thanksgiving had passed. Miss America farted into the microphone as if thereby to bear true witness to beauty, but that was only last season's attraction. No hero sums us up, no clown can contain us, and the Book of the People of the Book is in tatters.

So that what was lost at the end of each age was the image—not one to be discerned in water or fancied in clouds, but the image that inhered in the palpable One, letting it be at once paradigm of the Many and flesh of itself.

And so at the end of the day, the sky deepening as we walked back from the Prater, or home from the zoo, or along the river away from the fun-fair, the youngest child's balloon, the dark one, escaped from a fist tired at last, vanishing into its own element of the color between day and night.

Which the bandstand acknowledged in sweet conclusions, as horn and mellophone resolved their faintly crowded, adjacent *f* and *g* downward to *e* and *g,* firm in the faith that the ground was bearing up under them, making it seem that there had never been *f,* that thus it had ever been, healing, until the close of the soft cadence, the dominant wound.

VIOLET

At the song's beginning
Even as our voices
Rise we know the last words

And what it will sound like
To sing them at the end
Of the final burden;

Just so the cold fiddler
Hums the final chords of
Each of our capriccios

Even as he starts up.
But Jack, looking out of
The house that our song had

Him build, can see no cock
Crowing in the morn at
Break of ultimate day:

How then can we now shape
Our last stanza, furnish
This chamber of codas?

Here in the pale tan of
The yet ungathered grain
There may be time to chant

The epic of whispers
In the light of a last
Candle that may be made

To outlast its waning
Wax, a frail flame shaking
In a simulacrum

Of respiration. Oh,
We shall carry it set
Down inside a pitcher

Out into the field, late
Wonderers errant in
Among the rich flowers.

Like a star reflected
In a cup of water,
It will light up no path:

Neither will it go out.
Here at the easternmost
Edge of the sunset world

Starlings perch like quick notes
On a stave of wires high
Against the page of sky

But silently: in a
Mown oatfield what text will
The dallying night leave?

—A tree of light. A bush
Unconsumed by its fire.
Branches of flame given

Sevenfold tongue that there
Might be recompounded
Out of the smashed vessels

Of oil, of blood and stain,
Wine of grass and juice of
Violet, a final

White, here at the point of
Sky water and field all
Plunged in their own deep well

Of color whose bottom
Is all of the darkness.
If clear water is to

Give light, let it be here.
And if sound beyond breath
Of candle flame endure,

Then no wailful choir of
Natural small songs, no
Blend of winds; but let be

Heard their one undersong
Filling this vast chamber
Of continuing air

With the flickering of
Cantillation, quickened
Soon in the ringing dew.

Now, at the eastern edge of the black grass, he drinks a
draught of the juice of the last flower.

Ten black drops have been flung into the night, as if by his
little finger dipped into the deepest of cups;

And he considers the three higher colors that have been beyond color always; and he considers these at the dying of the wise light, remembering childhood:

In the chemist's window it was the same water that bubbled up through the differently colored glass tubes, even as oil streams forth into the lights, all the lights.

In the chemist's window, the hanging spheres of ruby, of emerald, of amber: he was told "Those are colored water" not as if a radiance had been selectively stained, but as if the colorless had been awakened from its long exile in mere transparency.

The diaspora of water ends when those colored bowls give back nothing that is untinted by their own light.

The eternities of the book end when there is only light for one eye, when the chant can be heard by only one ear: the hidden candle, the locked clavichord of implications.

Here they all were: The unfolding of What There Was
                      The warring of the leaves
                      The shaping of the rounded spore
                      And all that occurred therein
                      The opening of the codex
                      The echoes of wars, the shades of
                         shaping
                      And the shadows of the echoes of
                         the told told tales

They all end by the black grass, where fireflies dart about busily flickering with their hopeless fictions,

And the fiction that the first text was itself a recension of whispers, a gathering of what had been half-heard among the trees.

When morning comes, they will stop and go out, though morning will bring no light along the right-hand path on the margin of the dark.

It will be only his old man's dream of dawn that unrobes the violet, allows the early rose to take her morning dip.

He remembers this, and thinks not to quest among the regions of black for what lies beyond violet,

But would stay to hum his hymn of the hedges, where truth is one letter away from death, and will ever so be emended.

Blessed be who has crushed the olive for the oil.

Blessed be who has cracked the oil for the light.

Blessed be who has buried the light for the three tones beyond,

In which, when we have been stamped out and burned not to lie in the ashes of our dust, it will be to grow.

ON THE CALENDAR

T. 1:   I will start with an ancient trumpeting in my ears, an awakening in my eyes, as if the morning of a new month were a whole new year; but as my heart cries out under the burden of these surges of hope, the great call of the trumpet, the last call of all, will crack it. As if the end of the old were the end of the whole.

W. 2:   I will start a second time, awake again to an old alarm, move inevitably among the echoes of the previous day; in my family these things are always celebrated twice, and so I shall die once again of aggravated commencement.

Th. 3:   I will mount a high tower of speculation, away from which the plain of the immediate world will appear to roll, not so much inaccessible as undesired. Falling—as I lean out over that flattening of past, present and future as if to inspect it more closely but for no particular reason—I will not rise to meet my maker (even my last outcry will shrink from that), but will drop toward the mud from which I was made. Only at the end of my fall that clay will be kept from me by the unopened seal of the sidewalk.

F. 4:   I will eat crow, as usual, and gradually succumb to malnutrition.

S. 5:   I will put my foot into that part of life from which it is impossible to withdraw it.

Su. 6:   I will be holidaying in gross, comfortable Switzerland, and while walking by the lake in Geneva I will fall ill. Swiss Doctors will disagree about whether it is Tapanuli Fever or the Black Formosa Corruption, all the while I am too sick to be moved or even to protest.

M. 7:   I will rise to the ocean surface after diving under a very high breaking wave, pushing all-too-slowly up into the sweet, still darkness at the bottom of too deep a well.

T. 8:   I will wander into a picture gallery and this sort of thing will happen:

"Ilion Anagrammed in Oil: Agamemnon Destroyed" will make me age vastly overnight.

"The Mare of the Sea Heaves Her Vast Flanks along the Sands, or A Bad Dream of Lilith" will frighten me at night; awakening, my heart pounding, I will collapse, as I remember it, in something deeper than fear.

"Silver Quickening" will emit the cold gleaming of dead metal coming to life; it will chill me.

"Hewn out of the Head of Night" will turn me to stone.

W. 9:   I will sit in the darkening city, my desk lamp flooding the green blotter with its own color, cancelling all my obligations, debts, vows, commitments, resolutions, one by one. I will realize only at the last instant that I have gone too far, and confessed that the implicit assertion that I am alive was, after all, a lie.

Th. 10:   I will beat my breast in remorse so hard that it caves in.

F. 11:   I will choke on some bones of noon hidden in my soup of the evening.

S. 12:   I will discover a new continent: washed up on its beach, lying there naked and exhausted, the Princess of the Shore surrounding me with her laughing companions, I shall look up at her eyes into the smile of her father, the Lord of Hell.

Su. 13: I will enter a phase of erotic debauchery, searching among twisted regions of the Appalling for a hidden gateway into some sort of garden. Nothing will daunt me. And one calm evening of respite, I will pass into a pleasant glade of the more familiar sort of thing I had been fleeing in my explorations. Enjoying an elegantly turned-out and expensive one-legged daughter of joy, her stump tucked under my left arm for convenience in fucking, I shall succumb to a terminal transport which, given the relative absence of the uncanny, one could hardly have expected to be so strong.

M. 14: I will (a) tell a truth, (b) keep a promise and (c) dissolve away my bad faith, all incidentally and all unintentionally.

T. 15: I will enter a tabernacle in the wilderness of the city; the tabernacle, poorly built and tended, will collapse; ripe apples will drop upon my head, grapes will express themselves from bunches, falling like drops to the confused floor; a huge gray squash will crush my skull like a head.

W. 16: I will arrive at departure.

Th. 17: I will cut my finger on the sharp paper of my will while adding a new and whimsical codicil, and become infected.

F. 18: I will still be there, but everything else will have gone away.

S. 19: I will wander into a secluded part of the Central Park where three fourteen-year-olds, doubtless mistaking me for their true victim, Someone Else, will murder me for five dollars.

Su. 20: I will enter a warm, lamplit room where my father, sitting at his narrow desk over a page of log-ruled graph paper (on which the curves of increase get twisted into the lines of constancy), will look up at me and smile. His pen will be poised over the page. I will confide to him my childhood fear that he was, with sophisticated biochemical knowledge, gently and insistently poisoning me, through my food, toothpaste or mild medication. He will again reassure me, as he did in my childhood, laughing and surprised himself. And this time he will hand me, comfortingly, a poisoned drink.

M. 21: I will look in the mirror on my bedroom door and see myself from behind.

T. 22: I will write one bad line too many, it will reverse itself and, seizing the pencil from my affrighted fingers, proceed to erase all of me.

W. 23: I will join the other passengers in a slow bus as, after an eagle has flown at the windshield, causing the driver to lose control, the bus goes crashing down the lower slope of Mt. Parnassus, while other eagles wheel overhead.

Th. 24: I will take cold, finally.

F. 25: I will be three years old; I will turn a windy corner at the foot of an urban hill; an adult with a smile that I will not recognize at the time—that of a playmate with the same name as my yet unborn brother—will say "Hello!" and shoot me with a pistol.

S. 26: I will trip over a railroad tie in my dark bedroom and stub my soul.

Su. 27: I will awaken from a recurrent dream—of an unpleasant sort, but so familiar as to seem almost homely—to find myself in a low, narrow tunnel, along which I have been crawling, sharp rocks stabbing my knees and scraping my back, unable at last to move ahead or backward.

M. 28: I will issue forth, screaming, into my mother's tomb.

T. 29: I will receive from the new teller at the bank, a dim and inattentive person, a pair of strange coins made to fit perfectly over my closed eyelids; proving this by experiment, I will be hit by a large truck.

W. 30: I will attend a small party in my honor at which there will be three short girls of about seventeen, too shy to talk to me. One of them, very fat and with an almost deformedly large ass, will have so sweet and clear-skinned a face, such soft and bravely arranged hair, that my heart will break as I think of her and her isolation in and from her body. I will be found next morning in the deep snow.

Th. 31: I will pause before a shop window, long enough to see reflected in it a girl named Dot, with her name painted on her T-shirt, standing behind me awaiting recognition.

NOCTURNE

The great world turns
Cold of her own will, making stone
Of the hot heart, the rest slowly
Chilling even
Her skirts of dirt
Under which we have been mucking
About, rifling in their folds for
Flecks of gold. All of which causes
Her, enthroned in
Rock, to twitch the hem of her garb without a word.

Within the warm
Dark at the edge of the earth where
Vacancy of rock begins, we
Lie in the soft shadows of the sheets between us.
Through the windows comes the city
Light that is not
That of moon, nor yet the dark light
Of earth that will
Fall over our final length when height collapses.
It is the light in which we lie.

In the breadth of
Nightwind that shakes
The windowframes
A whisper has run out through the glass and become
The shattered lass of the courtyard,
Anna Mañana, clattering
Across shadows; round her shoulders a shawl of wind
Twitches; she sits waiting among
Dull bins and shining dark bags to
Regain a cold quondam body.

If the light lying across her
Lap makes her the Witch of Insinuation, then
We can only know her sister,
The bright Queen of Meaning, by her
Impalpability: in the clarity of
Daylight she is not to be seen,
But known by the radiance which is
Hers, giving back
What darkness keeps
Taking from us.

Call her Celia Manyhorses,
Indian giver: we remain in
Falling light, all that is left us,
Even for the eye that rises.
But this way of being unseen
Is not that of the most cloaked One:
Robed half in the glow of unbudded rose, half in
Blue too deep to read, beyond she dwells, but governs
Here and ever,
She who has arranged the marriage of dawn and death;

She whom we know by her iron
Chain, by her dry breath of what must
Be. It is she
Whom we have known all along, who prepared our dream
Of earth and breath;
She who leaves us
In the hard glare of morning with
Images out in the courtyard
Of dirt and wind,
Of what we are.

COLLECTED NOVELS

Where does one start? Perhaps here, at the middle
Of them all, as now, with *Elevenses,* that
Strange minor afterpiece, a book of partings
And mostly written on shipboard in passage
Between a new old world and an old new one,
Rocking between a fear of open ocean
And an arrival at a terror firmer
Than that, its separate sections somehow stand
For all the other novels: one can find them
There, such as in the scene where they both promise,
Standing by the inadequate lifeboat, drunk—

But you never read that one. Perhaps you did
Guess things about the juvenilia: *The
Rock Cried Out "I'm Burning Too"* was the first one
(In England called *A Universe of Death*), long,
Lyrical, assaulted by gangs of fancies,
Burdened with epigraphs, limping earnestly
Along corridors dimly lit with callow
Candor. On the other hand, *The Book of the
Perfect Clown,* the second of my first books, with
Its mock-dialogue form, inset tales, and arch
Picaro gestures, shone with counterfeit light.

Next, *My Brother's Reaper* was a mystery.
(I'd wanted its title to be *The Case of
The Limiting Case,* avowing how here the
Solution was indeed the discovery
Of the proof that the case was insoluble.)
It was an anatomy of doubt, and the
Successful but untriumphant detective
Disappeared unexplainedly at the end,
So that his career could not continue in

Other books, but only in life. Here it stands,
In all its cheap editions, with the others.

The truth is out. You have the books: I give you
Their true authorship. You'll find among them our
Collaboration, the epistolary
Most Said, about the couple who put about
Experimental rumors of their life in
Order to trace out the modellings of truth
(Keeping safe in that the facts were notional)
By friends and lovers. And about what happened to
Them thereby (we rejected *The French Letters*
As title, with "For Prevention of Disease
Only" as epigraph—but you remember . . .)

It does belong with the others—even with
That purgatorial vision, *Peeping Tom,*
Its solipsistic opposite, lonely and
Mad in its questing for certainties of light;
The intricate *récit* of an old voyeur
Epistemologist, it tells of his three
Wives, Virgilia, Matilda and Beatrice,
His three lives with them, and of his going blind
After a life of seeing wisely and far
Too well; full of long digressions on mirrors,
Cameras, pictures—not the best sort of novel.

No: the few good ones were those which went about
Their sad work of imagining marriages,
Doing what we need such texts for, providing
Models of the mysteries of pairs we are
Not part of, and mirrors of our unknown own.
Leaving, for one, and *The Right Links* and even
Merrydown, that romance of sunken heights and
Afterpleasures: broad canvases, cities and
Seaside sojourns, many households, and, that there

Be truth, humming swarms of irrelevancies—
These redeemed the early games and drawn-out songs.

The novel of wartime London, *Dark Cremorne,*
Hardly a failure, dwelt in its retractions
Of vision—squinting through magnesium glare,
Turning emptied eyes toward the cold dawn—and was
One with its minima—few characters, a
Minor rondo of fewer locales, even
The poor, grey wartime paper of the book James
Chamberlain was reading, sad food, those frightful
Knickers to be got past to delicate hairs.
Yet these simple, enviable pleasures robbed
From death seem bright idylls of denial now.

(No, *Blackbird Cross* would have been a bad title
—Taken from the bus-route terminus and, of
Course, from Helen Elizabeth's dream: you must
Have guessed by now what part you played in it.) But
About the destroyed manuscripts of what was
To have been *Jealousy* I shall say nothing.
It is not here among the works. It might have
Been the worst or the best—a vivisection
Of desperate knowledges and narrowings,
Of the sense that one's death is being kept from
One—or one's life. The earliest drafts were endless.

They are finally together on the shelf—
As if about to be packed up for moving—
Here at a somber time of dissolution,
Leaning wearily against each other: some
From out of the closet and still dusty with
Concealment, some that had been staring out at
You all along, others from scattered regions
Of the house, huddling together, refugees
Bereft if not of their titles then of their

Various makers' names—the ones in which I
Penned them (or in which I, too, was penned). All mine.

Having no terror of design, you would not
Have dreaded knowing that all these works had one
Author. But that I failed to write them under
My true name is not a matter merely for
The spirit's connoisseurship: to gather them
Here, half a dusty sheaf of hybrid grains, is
To acknowledge the too early arrival
Of frost, the race for a few last hours of light
To read by, to plant or reap by. I would have
Given you their common life: I have left you
Them, though, like eleven expired leases:

The last one, in press, being *Some Natural
Tears,* which we were to have read together, hand
In hand. You may perhaps now guess its subject—
The old story we all know and can never
Comprehend, its fierce transfers of elation
Across the bound of loss, its presentiments
Of endings, departures in the evening
Shade of sky and distant horizontal woods.
Announced in this reprint of *Elevenses,*
It shall at least reach you under my own name.

THE LADY OF THE CASTLE

Venus Pudica stands, bent. Where her hand is
Cupping her marble mound a mystery has
Come into being as the sculptor hides what
    Stone could not show yet,

Nor bronze expound. The goddess may be guarding
Herself, or in a special mode of pointing
Out (should we call it "curving in"?) her temple,
    Teaching her children

The central and precious, where they may be found.
Or indeed, as the girls say, she is hiding
Nothing, nor instructing—she is caressing
    That which she barely

Touches, warming those feelings which for her are
Wisdom blossoming even within marble.
What her maker buried she loves, and thereby
    We are revealed it.

Far in the minimal North, some contracted
Hand or eye has carved into senseless clunch an
Impudent and schematic presence, done in
    Primal intaglio,

A circle head perched on a larger circle
Of lady body, spidery legs drawn up
And outward showing off on the church tower
    Under the clock, and

Cut in a sort of Linear C, her slit.
Her hands touch nothing but her knees held open.
It is not she who joys in it, nor teaches;
    But from beneath her

A very well-hung personage indeed is
Climbing up toward her, as if far from having
Merely no words for things, their sculptor had no
    Method of using

Images for them: no things, only actions.
And thus translated into language her wedge
Would be a "Let's-get-up-on-her-and-in-there."
    Hieroglyphic

Of nature's own cuneiform, she sits high
But almost hiding in the irrelevance
Of a religious building now to the young
    Mums of the village.

Ignored, then, or misread by mythographers
—Myopically concluding that a corpus
Christi lies beneath a bungled cross—as a
    Crude Deposition,

She with her terrible thin cut is not to
Be any the less feared by those who read signs
And remember instances of their wide truths
    Narrowed in darkness:

Hers is the closed door into the stone again.
The soft traps having long since sprung, the marble
Self-adoring dolls long crumbled, hers is the
    Linear kingdom.

THE ANGLER'S STORY

I let down my long line; it went falling; I pulled. Up came
A bucket of bad sleep in which tongues were sloshing about
Like frogs and dark fish, breaking the surface of silence, the
Forgetfulness, with what would have been brightness in any
Other element, flash of wave, residual bubbling,
But were here belches of shadow churned up by the jostling
Tongues from the imageless thick bottom of the heavy pail.
I could not reach into that fell stuff after them, nor fling
Them back into night like inadequate fish; nor would they
Lie flat and silent like sogged leaves that had been flung under
Mud, but burbled of language too heavy to be borne, of
Drowned inflections and smashed predications, exactness pulped
Into an ooze of the mere desire to utter. It was
My bucket, and I have had to continue to listen.

AFTER AN OLD TEXT

His head is in the heavens, who across the
Narrow canyon of pillow from yours harkens
With gazing hand and hearing knees through darkness,
    Looking and listening

To the sweet quietude of terminating
Conversation, the gentle brief wake for the
Long-dead day, the keening of his shortened
    Breath on your shoulder:

This revision of you sucks out the sound of
Words from my mouth, my tongue collapses, my legs
Flag, my ears roar, my eyes are blind with flame; my
    Head is in hell then.

LOOKING EAST ON TWELFTH STREET

On an afternoon "of extraordinary splendour and beauty"
The late, blue sky pours into the jagged mold
Of buildings racing down the street toward a vanishing point.
Houses are bright above and reassuringly shadowed
Below, and "clarity" no longer needs to mean
Unfuzziness, as it does, but regains its old sense
Of famous brightness; so that the view straight across town,
Lit by a sun who has skipped back behind one to see
His work from a distance, is a look into something inside
A theatrical preparation like the holes
Cut into the back of the world at Palladio's
Theatre in Vicenza. But it is for the solitary
Rambler of avenues to read in passing, this illustration
On a turning page of a passage from earlier
In the book when there were to have been two figures
Receding down the sidewalk to join the shaded
Part of the scene. Their walking would have been joyful, their
Disappearance at the end a sign that they had been welcomed.
The perspective is correct only for a moment
Of walking by, for the eye that aims north of that scrapes
The cracked sidewalks below with the wet point of its gaze.

From In Place

THE WAY WE WALK NOW

It was not that there were only the old ways of going from one chamber to another: we had learned to imitate the noble walk of those who had built, and dwelt in, the Great Palaces, moving gravely through the interconnecting rooms; aware of the painted ceilings and the import of the images there for their lives, but never needing to look up at them; free among their footmen; roaming their spaces and yet by no means imprisoned in the fragile grandeur to which, in the afternoon light, the rooms had fallen. We had learned thereafter to mock that stiff way of walking, and after that, to replace it with our own little dances and gallops; we roller-skated from room to room, or occasionally bicycled. Being confined by the layout was not the point, nor was it what may or may not have happened to the houses—whether they were indeed in ruins or merely in need of repair. We had all gone away somewhere: off to war, or to the city, or had shipped out for the East. And those of us who returned, or who had stayed wherever it was, came quite naturally to go about in the field, or among the hills or through the streets. At first, it was almost with memorized maps of the ways rooms opened off each other, and of just what courts it was on which the various windows gave; after that, with no recollected plan, but always moving the better for having started out in one of the great houses.

But then it almost ceased to matter where we were. What had become necessary that we do by way of amble, or of hop skip and jump, had so taken over power from mere place that it generated the shapes of space through which it moved, like a lost, late arrival at the start of a quest who had set out nonetheless, dreaming each new region into which he wandered. Pictures of the old places still had a certain pathos; but they were not of ourselves or of our lives. The distance that had been put between us and the houses crammed full of chambers was utter, like that between the starry heavens above and the text below us, on the opened page.

A WEEK IN THE COUNTRY

A plague raged in the city. In a region nearby, August fields were shivering under a very heavy rain, but for hours before, the grasshoppers' buzzings had crowded into any ear that could not escape listening, and the high, soft thunder had been as easy to ignore as the rumors relayed by Rube and Boob, the turnip farmers over the hill, and as boring. In the house, a trapped wasp sang madly in the windowpane, and softly butted the narrow glass with a sound that was always on the edge of echoing a familiar noise. But there is no story to tell: Village life had broken down and the solitary heroisms of the simple women in their flowering yards had faded into darkening pages. The farms yielded their cash crops. Those who huddled in the house during the long rain, and rekindled the stubs of blue candle until there was power again, were not going to tell old stories to pass the time as they sorted odd seeds in what light there was, or silently sat out the important thunder. It was as if they could not be prelude to any narrative that would not be twisted out of shape as it awkwardly side-stepped the embarrassments of its own unfolding, or strove to avert its hearing from the creaking of hinges as its own doors opened and shut. It was as if sheer place, unable to act, reigned nonetheless, at a noble distance from what, were it nearer, would be a foreground, and as if its genius lay in this.

ABOUT THE HOUSE

In the high attic, all the old things had been accumulating meaning. Down in the basement were the pump, the furnace, the oldest masonry, the dark bottles of Pomerol settling slowly toward their prime. The difficulty of living in the house, in all the rooms between these, lay partially in trying to understand how moving up and down stairs between the floors was only a matter of changing levels, not of achieving any real elevation. There were forays made up to all the dusty hangings, the closed chests whose labels themselves, covered with dust, seemed to require labeling, the old pictures that looked somewhat grotesque as opposed to the remembered versions of them with which we were conversant downstairs. When there were descents down the cellar steps, it was because something was wrong, or something was being retrieved; we moved up into the spaces under the eaves, however, when there was nothing else to do. On the floors between, the significance of everything was one with its use.

Stepping out-of-doors—on an October afternoon, perhaps, whose brightness and touches of chill kept the edges of everything very clear—and looking back at the house from outside was something else again: anything it could lead us to conclude would be like a tale told by an abandoned house to some passer-by, who, if he retained any of the whole matter, would remember the interiors, the rooms, the passageways, which he had visualized from the story. He should have forgotten what the house looked like about which he had stopped on his walk to inquire. This is also somehow involved with the problems of living there.

KEEPSAKES

Only after eighteen years had passed was it possible to regard the
bed and the three bullets in any relation at all to each other and to
what had been decaying around them. A man had died in the bed,
which was broad and strong and costly, and his widow gave it to the
energetic friends. The bullets were small, heavy, .32 caliber cartridges,
the clip that had held them long since lost, the enabling pistol long
since sold by the widow, who had forgotten the last three cartridges.
The energetic friends removed them for safekeeping, meaning to
deal with them later on, with the effect that for years and years they
rattled inside desk drawers, among staples and scissors, or in little
boxes of paper or tin or leather. Their brass cases and copper noses
grew dull. As they lost luster, they seemed to lose their meaning as
objects, as if no concept could adhere to them, as if something
inherent had leaked out of them and then perhaps dried from off
their surfaces.

So that the problems posed by what they actually were—whether
age had incapacitated them, and so forth—and by what they had
been, and might be, for, ceased to seem pressing or even interesting.
The only appropriate way of dealing with them consisted eventually
in visiting them in whatever container they happened to occupy;
handling them; perhaps even from time to time momentarily
misplacing one or two, so that a short, nervous search had to ensue
before one of them, duller than could have been expected, turned up
at the end of a dark drawer. That they were those particular bullets,
that there were three of them, that they were not exactly a legacy
but had to be coped with nonetheless after their owner's death—these
insistent and unimpressive facts inhered in their weight and in
their familiar appearance, in the way they would lie rhyming like
one-word lines, two of them parallel, the third slightly askew but
with its tip touching the others. All this naturally obscured how
during all that time they may have been acquiring an enormous
importance of their own.

The bed and the widow entered a world of narrative, however. Just where this world touched that of the bullets—and, by inference, where these regions lay and still lie in relation to one another—is not easily perceived. One can imagine thinking, as he put on his spanking new solar topee, of the curves and returns of a dark river working through rain forest. One can think of previous encampments, of the traces of earlier explorations. And then there would be the narrative world itself. The first glimpse of it might come at sunset along the river, with lights beginning to appear at what might be a border station. And then one would begin to know what had gone on—not, surely, the events themselves (the widow remarried, then left her husband for new sadnesses, the bed consumed the lives of the energetic friends who lay in it until they fell apart) but the processes whereby one's things can objectify, can shrink as the moisture of ceremony leaves them for the general air.

In other words, the bed had always lain midway between the bullets and the widow, as if it were a text, neither person nor object. The widow might evaporate into hearsay. The bed was clearly becoming more and more like the bullets. And the bullets, dulled now to a final low tone past which they would not move, lay in whatever box it was, creating more and more of their own purity.

END OF A CHAPTER

... But when true Beauty does finally come crashing at us through the stretched paper of the picturesque, we can wonder how we had for so long been able to remain distracted from its absence.

THE OLD PIER-GLASS

It was as if, he thought, someone had censored the whole of a well-meaning but naïvely loquacious wartime letter, leaving about its cut-out center only a frame to be sent on nevertheless, with needless earnestness, to its addressee. Alas, it was even more as if the letter had announced a death to begin with, and only the black borders and a little white, by way of a mat within them, were left. For there was in fact no glass in the old, heavily lacquered frame. The carved wood surrounded only the dusty corner of the corridor it stood in.

This in itself neither amused nor frightened him. But what if he had had to consider a pair of mad brothers, clad in identical nightgowns, fake moustaches and tasseled caps, looking out at each other from either side of the empty mirror-frame? He would have had to contemplate a trope of imaging, of presence making creakingly do for the pictures that are usually dragged in to replace whatever is absent. It would be a matter of a person replacing a lost replacement. Very, very funny at first, it would have to come to him, this time, very fearfully indeed.

AFTER FLOOD DAMAGE

(Start with the sound of the brook) The sound of the brook was as insistent as a hissing of nearby fire, and it cut such a broad swath of audibility through the trees, that it swallowed up, and made part of its own utterance, whatever those agitated branches had to whisper. Which was much, but which was not about much. *(Go on about the trees)* The tale each pale-tongued leaf had to tell in response to the wind's mindless and bullying catechism was no more than a catalogue of complaints about that questioning. *(Mindless? bullying?)* The wind was not of this place, had not dwelt here long enough to play on the instrument of the given. *(What about the water in the brook, then?)* A different matter: the nymphs of rock had always been here, and their films and veils and draperies were the sole and proper emanations of their visibility. Or say that they possessed the passing waters, while our poor leaves, multitudinous and weak, were claimed by the nightriding rushes of wind. *(Well then, what did the sounds of the water mean? what did the brook say?)* None of us knew at the time, but that did not untune the quality of our attention. *(So that one is to end with the sound of the brook?)* One is to end with the sound of the brook.

CROCUS SOLUS

A sigh? No more: a yellow or white rupture of the cold silent
winter ground, the exclamation of such effort. Yet unaccompanied
by the echoing multitudes that hope surveys; one only, and whether
an accident or an example, too important in its uniqueness to be
considered important for its meaning. O, spring will come, and
one time it will not, but what we are to know we will know from
all the various emblems crying, out of the grass, *vivace assai*, and
waving in the soft wind, *ô Mort*. One swallow of water makes no
summer of earth. One drop of darkness is no sign of wine. One
flower points to nothing but itself, a signboard bravely hung outside
the signpainter's. The crocus of all points, lying along the river,
that speak for themselves is but one point of saffron or of snow.
A sign? O, more . . .

SOMETHING WRONG DOWN AT THE POND

One summer evening when the sky behind him was still red with
the remains of daylight, and the small green heron was making
sponking noises from across the pond, he came down to the
motionless water. He stood at the edge and peered over the reeds
through which the wind groped hesitantly, not so much toward
music as away from stillness. He saw emerging from a shadow in the
water, framed by the infirm brightness of what, by inference, was
reflecting the heavens, a head. He moved: it moved; he tilted his
head toward his right shoulder: the image did, in its reversed way,
likewise. And so: and so; and more: and more—until the rhythm
of action and recognition gradually began to slough off its false
resemblance to cause and effect, and just before the water darkened
into a condition below reflectiveness, the handsome youth realized
with an ambiguous thrill that it was indeed the head in the pool
which was reflected by the figure that was his own. It was not
tragic to discover that he was the image of something more
substantial than himself, something even less accessible to his elicited
reach toward it than a fragile fiction floating in water might be to
a desiring hand. It was rather comforting to be absolved of the
responsibility of taking on either Knowledge or anything serious
in the way of Fate. Night closed in on the pond, making the
matter of the images deeply moot.

IN PLACE OF BODY

The garden is a very singular one. It is not that it is difficult of access—although one is constantly told that there is only one way in, there are in fact many—but that this contingent availability is of its essence. A public garden, a private park—each of these not despite the other, but because of it. This place is always said to contain representations of the absent forms: branches of the oldest trees intertwine in the touches of marriage survived; vines embrace their props, not with the deadly cuddling of some ground-cover that has run to stifling excesses, but with the old grace of taking and giving support; stalks of flower push out through the earth, filling the holes they make and mixing root and matrix into an element of ground; the evening air caresses the soft curves of the turf. But as if this were not enough, the lap of the ground cradles a body of delight, the representation fitted to its primary form, the hills of the body embedded in the valleys of the shade. It is as if every word here were embracing the object it named. And then meaning would flourish, whether in absence or presence being of no matter now.

FIGURES OF SPEECH. FIGURES OF THOUGHT. FIGURES OF EARTH AND WATER.

Once upon a time, the old, wild synecdoche of landslides was frighteningly transumed when a mountain—Mt. Black—rolled downward like one of its own boulders, over the whole peaceless land. In metonymy meanwhile, beyond the other mountains, a mad sea was flowing somewhere, like a river.

THE BOAT

It took him away on some nights, its low engine running silently on even until he was too far out to hear it himself. It was as dark as the elements of water and night through which it moved. It was built for one: he was helmsman and supercargo both. It rode so low that he could roll into it from wherever it was tied up, and lie prone, his head perhaps turned to port. It responded surely and delicately to the controls, all accessible from where he lay. It headed out, but never back: he could not remember having come ashore from it. It was out of service for some years, after which he came to realize that his final ride on it, some night, would not be unaccompanied, that the boatman on that voyage would stay aboard, and that he himself would disembark at last.

OVER THE HILLS AND FAR AWAY

The wind had blown his hair about and then gone on to inquire among the remaining leaves on the trees behind him. Otherwise, the rise of ground on which he stood was bare—rock, whitish grass, cold earth: these and the gray of the sky were as frames for each other, the conditions of picturing without a picture, presentations of presentations but with no meaning to be transferred. But what he saw as he looked toward the horizon was another matter. The scene pictured itself; the hills, the sky poured down among them, the breaks in the clouds all glossed the statement of sheer distance. The wind returned and whistled a refrain among the grasses: it was the only tune that it could play. He had taken up a place in which he could come to terms with the lie of the land.

THE DANCING SHADOWS

A walker along the half-lit avenues that night would most
probably have noticed nothing unusual as he moved amongst the
returning throngs, thinned out somewhat by the raw weather and
the emergence of the late hour from the bustle of the day's end.
Dropping snow softened the yellow light that fell across the sidewalk,
meaninglessly, from grim and glaring lamps. One walker perceived
the multiplicity of his shadows in this kind of light: they lengthened,
shortened, blended, superimposed themselves upon each other's
paling ghosts, and generally made light of the power of one's
shadow over one's substance. How they danced with each other,
these mere images, before they vanished in the caverns of flat snow
opened up by other lights! Like all the other walkers, and the
dexterous snowflakes, and the cars moving by down the avenue in
the other direction, the shadows of shadow were all part of the
poetry of here and there. Neither sacred to this place, nor totally
accidental to it.

NOT SOMETHING FOR NOTHING

What he had begun only lately to notice was this: that he had always noticed relatively little of what was going on inside of, and among, the things he encountered; and this led him to recall noticing always what he had already possessed himself of: shining objects of memory. So that when, for example, he passed by something growing, something that had or had not bloomed yet, he would have had to wander back into the bright mountain meadow all ringed about with high pines and where all the names grew, to pluck a flower of designation and bear it back, through the shadowy woods, to the spot of attention. And it was because he could notice so little that he was able to call attention to things so startlingly sometimes. His mind was always wandering. He could point the way home.

PATCHES OF LIGHT LIKE
SHADOWS OF SOMETHING

—So that we have, after all, to be grateful that our light lies
broken in pieces: were we to have to live in the generality of it,
without the beneficence of the shady (no matter how questionable
now, always), it would be unbearable. Perhaps if everything
were to be reconstituted along with it, perhaps if the flashes of
acknowledgment so scattered among us were finally to be reconvened,
we might manage it all. But as it is, the very breaking-up of the
radiance that might have for ever remained a deep ground was
what will always cause us to have embraced these discrete fragments—
turning on and off, fading, ending in a border of darkness—as
with the arms of our heart.

A VIEW OF THE RUINS

A short walk up from the hotel brings one to a place more than half way up, from which the whole site is visible and the different areas more discernible than from their midst. Toward the left, an ancient grove will appear to throw shadows more substantial looking than the trees themselves. The cool colonnade seems even from such a height to echo with long-departed footsteps; across from it, the stoa may be perceived, with its rather boring porch. An ancient upended tub (to the right of the stoa) is still inhabited by dogs. Nearby was the tasteful garden. The whole place was once busy with meaning and the bustle of life, and when one looks over the whole matter from above, the various areas can seem to have been plausibly engaged with the living day. It is only from among the excavations that the point seems lost—indeed, as the local saying goes, "The overview, lest nothing be overlooked!" As to what these ruins have to do with our lives, our problems and headaches, our terrors and representations, each traveler will of course determine for himself.

A HOUSE IN THE TROPICS

New York. Cold. Cold everywhere. Cold in all the warm places.
Cold in the interstices between adjacent blocks of cold. Cold at the
heart of cold, and at the heart of the word "cold", and at the cold
heart of the word "everywhere". But no—somewhere there is a dream
of warming, and out of the warm blue comes a slow interisland
steamer, visiting palm-ringed bays, putting off one sort of goods and
taking on another, going from port to port much as one might
proceed, errantly, from adventure to adventure without being aware
of the cycle of tasks they comprised. And once launched into that
heat, one might move from dream of place to dream of place, from
house to house, without suspecting that there was a final one that
one had been inevitably approaching. The House of Shells, full of
ornaments so gorgeous that one never tried, before moving on, to
listen to them; the House of Fruit, where warmth and sweetness
dwell in a mild way; the House of Distance which, to whatever
island one came, was always there, even if only as a low,
unprepossessing hut. (On some islands, this was locally thought
of as the House of Place Itself, but this resulted from an ancient
linguistic error.) It was not that, down there, things and places
resembled each other more, but that the warm climate did something
to their modes of signifying. Their ways of meaning what they did,
these places, were comely.

MEMORIES OF THE GRAND TOUR

I was young then, of course, and could not know what it all meant, even though delight and instruction ran joyfully together along the boulevards, down the dark passages and out onto the hot, bright, silent squares. Else I should have recorded the whole journey in all of its continuing life; it is not, you see, to be revived in any way, and can only schematically—and perhaps thereby somehow horribly—be reconstructed from the pictures. (I mean those accomplished water-color sketches that travelers would learn to make, less like snapshots than like guarded time exposures, souvenirs rather than recollections; but no matter.) What I am left with even now is only the sense of moving from place to place, savoring each one the while thinking of the portion of the journey that yet lay ahead. I think now—but did not remember at the time—of my childhood: at the movies on Saturday afternoons, the light from the screen is reflected on my face, halfway through the Western, feeling the pleasure of the moment and the more prudently taken delight in the feeling of the remainder of the film, the shorts, the gangster movie, all yet to come, all still unconsumed.

And so it was with this: the high point of beginning at the place of the clear pools, the color of the sky and of ancient wisdom. Then the shells of the sounding beach; after that, the trek inland to the speaking well of the oracle, below the long, fragrant hill. Then I came, as one usually did, to the promontory below which lay the long reach of the whole land—the beautiful hills, the curving plain below that reached down to the forested area and the hidden mound. It was never purely the pleasure of the moment, nor the anticipatory joy of what one would reach next and next after that. It was the gradually unfolding nature of the entirety that could make one take so seriously such a conventional old trip, even though that unfolding would only be perceived long afterward, when the entirety could be completed because finally and fully imagined, rescued from the cold gaol in which failing memory, in her filthy smock, caressed and clucked over the fractured pieces.

ASYLUM AVENUE

Here is a region through which you move, yet which moves through you as you make your *paseo*. It is as if it were receptive to the space you bring along with you, and as if all the spaces flowed into each other like clear, green water. It is itself a wide walk past heavily meaningless cars and their motion, descending in curving and gracious declines into the business of being a street. Yet it never needs to become a mere boulevard, broadly proclaiming itself over buried and forgotten bulwarks, but remains the extension of what it comes toward, which itself kindly advances to meet what has been moving forward at it for so very long. It is the neighborhood of points of refuge through which you pass: they continually astonish you with their inventiveness; with the manner in which food and drink have been tucked away in them; with the devices by which you may see and not be seen. And suppose that there was an encounter to be had there (I think of a recently dead friend appearing at your door, his arms full of books and papers, in place of someone else you had invited, cheerfully assuring you that the reports of his sudden death in Italy were quite mistaken)—it would be as much part of your walk as your very setting out. It would not be occasional. Nor would the sidewalk along the asphalt shore constitute a road. It would be a way of getting to work.

BUILDING A TOWER

It is because of what one has not found—a tan silo pushing up beside the gambrel roof of a stone barn; a square, ruined tower, Frankish, stone, backed on a pine grove and overlooking the hot sand toward the calm blue water; a dark, shingled cupola inspecting the wild, gray sea; an unused wooden water-tank atop a penthouse facing westward beyond the park; an obsolete lighthouse near the mouth of the bay—of what one has not been able to adapt, that one has to build. One can plan and plan for years, but in the end the finished structure will always remain somewhat surprising: it will have to seem, always, to have been come upon, in a middle distance, from a dark walk, the wanderer enwrapped in his study of the failing light and what arises within it. It will always have to keep its own distant appearance: even as one looks out, after years of keeping it, through one after another of the windows—toward the fire of sunset, out across the noon fields, into the cold rain dripping from bare boughs—there must be at least one window, however narrow, out of which one can see what one looks toward the tower for. One must be amid all that—dark books shadowing the interior walls, bright vineyards lying toward the river outside—amid what has always been, and will be, beyond.

IN PLACE OF PLACE

First of all, the original enclosure within which was our everywhere: it became, when we had to leave it, nowhere that was or was not to be. All the places we would have we would also have to take not as recompense, but just as images which eternity can nurture. Even if we could gather them all together, they would not compose what was less merely image; their designatum—the lost spot for which all our locations stand—would go on being merely what it is. As, for example, pain—piercing, throbbing or flickering— is a trope for the knowledge of that spot which we could not leave unplucked.

Well, then, to recapitulate: the earliest places are all taken away—the bright morning beach and the reddening late sand; the small stark sickroom; the caves in the merry rocks of childhood, the upright piano that loomed high above; all the Kinderscenen *inscribed in Albums for the Old. Nothing is given back; it is only that everything follows, making a kind of replacement in time. The space of these places has gone away, leaving only room for representations. The places that follow, far ones and near, momentary and familiar, are themselves representations: of the lost places? Yes. Of people? Perhaps. Of ourselves? Usually.*

So that everywhere we visited, every area wherein we may have been said to dwell, turned out in time to be bases we had had to touch, acceptances of what the world, madly gesturing as we moved about it, may have meant by its unagreed-upon signals. Every valley was also a picture of somewhere else we had not yet been to; each monument we climbed to the top of went away and left room to be remembered, but the memory would always fill up another space, the site of its late blossoming.

And, finally, there is something right about the vagrancy of the replacements. Nowhere can keep us for too long. Let us look at it this way: for want of the fruit the garden was lost, for want of the garden the places were gained, for want of the places new places arrived, for want of new places we dreamed and we dreamed. We composed in the tiniest inner room all the chambers of the endless palace, opening on to each other, directly as well as indirectly, off unlit corridors, once entered and left, then lost, even if returned to at a later time and by a route that we could never have known to be circuitous. And each room a place of mistakenness, so much so that while we are in it, there is no way of getting it right. Once left, there is only what we say of it, which is never mistaken.

There must be some way of learning from this about the last replacement, which is not of picture for place nor of place for picture; which is not like filler, unpainted terra-cotta smoothed into the space between places—interrupting the line of the dancer's drapery but not feigning, with a curious false art, where it was to go; which is not, in fact, anything occupying any space at all. Nor is it a matter of everywhere becoming empty space, waiting patiently—and with whatever wisdom was supposed to have been a version of—to be occupied by the new everywhere again. It is the replacement of space itself, of that space within which place has its being, with what will never again leave room.

From Tales Told
of the Fathers

THE HEAD OF THE BED

for Robert Penn Warren

*At the mountainous border of our two countries there is a
village; it stands just below a pass, but some of the older
houses lie higher up along the road, overlooking more of
the valley than one might think. The border has never
been heavily guarded, and our countries are peaceful.
Theirs lies beyond the pass; in the other valley a large village looks up toward the mountains and toward us. The
border itself is marked only by an occasional sign; but then
there is the Trumpeter. His clear, triadic melodies break
out through the frosty air, or through the swirling mists.
From below, from above, the sound is commandingly
clear, and it seems to divide the air as the border divides
the land. It can be heard at no fixed intervals, and yet with
a regularity which we accept, but cannot calculate. No one
knows whether the Trumpeter is theirs or ours.*

I

Heard through lids slammed down over darkened glass,
Trees shift in their tattered sheets, tossing in
Shallow sleep underneath the snoring wind.

A dream of forests far inside such sleep
As wakeful birds perched high in a dread wood,
Brooding over torn leaves, might mutter of

Rises over the pain of a snapped twig
That ebbs and throbs not with a shore rhythm
But with the pulsings of dark groves—as if

A bird of hurting swept over hooded
Places, fled, and at intervals returned—
Clocked by the broken aspirates roaring

Along their own wind, heard within their wood,
Their own deep wood, where, fluttering, first words
Emerge, wrapped in slowly unfolding leaves.

2

Where, where, where? Where is here? Where is Herr Haar,
Tendrils lashing across the light his eyes
Open on, Joker of Awakening?

Where is where? Where the cracked suddenness wide
On that frail wall, where amber filigree
As of an egg's marble vein his pillow;

Where webby vines clinging coldly to his
White eyeball fall away to dust; where hair
Hangs across the world, here is where. And there

Is the acknowledging skull of far wall—
Two hollow, shaded windows and a smudge
Of dark mirror between. And there is here

No light. Not yet. Deep in the woods' heart, soft,
Dim leaves close up again; heat lightning rips
Pallid sheets, silent, across roughened sky.

3

Floor lamps and their shadows warmed the room where
He lay dead in bed; and then the windows
Were thrown open to admit of the night.

Exhalations of buses rose hoarsely
Over the reservoir's onyx water
Beaded about with lights, an appalling

Brooch clutching the appalling shawl of the
Dark park through whose trees no relieving wind
Blew. No zephyr sniffed the window curtains

Pushing through the stuff of outer silence
That cars coughed in; only an old great-aunt
Waited, on her nightly visitation,

Denied again by his awakened, dark
Blood, as come bubbling up bone-gathering
Trumpetings of unscheduled, sombre cocks.

4

Slanting, lean, gray rain washing the palace
Steps floods the inner court: Vashti mutters
There, dripping among her ancillaries,

Of displeasure, loss, and now a cold walk
To distant parts of the palace, gutters
Roaring with possibilities, water

Burbling the Ballade of All the Dark Queens—
Not the wet abjects, but those who yet reign
(*Where is Lilith?*) in that they could refrain—

Not Hagar sent out among the dry rocks,
But Orpah opting for hers, and Martha
Answering her own hearth and electing

The bubbling merriment of her pudding,
Reading the night-girl Lilith's name in white,
Vanishing from her windy, drying sheets.

5

Coarse breath fanning the closed air by his ear
Stirred up the swarming night-bees who had been
Honeying nearby, where faces blossomed

Out of the darkness, where creepers mingled
With long, low-lying trunks, humming among
Damp hollows, herding and gathering there,

But unheard by him undreaming, by him
Beamed in upon by the wide moon who smeared
Light here and there into dark surfaces—

Madam Cataplasma, her anointment
Vast, her own outstretched form fantastic there
Beside him, as if on awakening

A filthy myth of Lilith would lie spilled
Like darkness on the sheet of light. He rolled
Out of this bad glade and slept darkly on.

6

He felt his hand feeling another hand
Feeling his own: staring up after a
Fly's noisiness, his bony image lay

Where he was beside himself, imbedded
In the nearby, the space readied and wide
And yawning, fed up with the emptiness

Of its tents, rags of cloudy percale hung
Over bumps and hummocks. It shaded them,
He and he lying and listening while

Kicked fabric fell softly over their bones.
Sighing settles: toward what does buzzing fly?
About what does the sound of breathing dream?—

An echo fleeing down twisted halls; a
Buzzing fly rising over him and his
Like something bland and vague deserting them.

7

Down the shaded street, toward an avenue
Of light, a gleaming picture receded:
The sudden lady, tall, fair and distant

Glided slowly, and her beautiful leg
Sole but unlonely, swung walking along
Between the companionable crutches,

Flesh hand in hand with sticks. He followed them
And waited in a sunny place, and when
She halted, there were woods. Turning her head,

She smiled a bad smile, framed by a shadow
Flung from a tower somewhere. He dared not move
Toward her one leg, toward her covered places

Lest he be lost at once, staring at where
Lay, bared in the hardened moonlight, a stump
Pearly and smooth, a tuft of forest grass.

8

The Hyperboreans gathered him up
And bore him across, out of the shadows,
Into their realm of tenderness where there

Is room enough, but where there are no gaps
Between the seeding and the gathering;
Nor wintering, in which recovering

Desire grows in its caves, nor the buzz
Of endless August, golden, deified:
No need for these. In that bland land he lay—

Envisioning frost and fallen silver,
Half hearing the cricket in the parching
Oat-straw, feeling tears from his weeping brow,

Dreaming of intervals lost—stretched out on
Wastes not of snow, nor sand, nor cloud, he tossed,
And knew not why, in that undying noon.

9

Leaving that unfair, seasonless land was
More than a traverse of uneasiness;
More than an antlike file over glacial

Sheets and then, at last, across the fold of
Pass, pausing above a final valley
Shining in a new light, and shivering

At the approach of strange, dark guards; more than
Their distrust, and their icy moustaches
Masking frowns at our tokens of passage

(He held a light bulb, heavy in his right
Pocket, and they, red stones in their left ones)
More than making one's way; and returning

Over a way not yet gone over, hurt
Like first smashings of light, shrunk to a lamp
Shaded, grim, sun-colored at four A.M.

10

Beyond the cold, blue mountain and beyond
That, we shall wander on the pale hills when
Shadows give over bending along the

Slopes, and the silent midday light, unchanged
For hours and days, is pierced only by our
Two moving specks, only by the cricket's

Warm humming. Then, what we hear becoming
What we see, the gray; the wind enclosing;
The poplars' breath; the sad, waiting chambers.

Will there have been room? There will have been room
To come upon the end of summer where
Clustered, blue grapes hang in a shattered bell,

Or there, in a far, distant field, a swarm
Of bees in a helmet, metal yielding
Honey, balmy drops glistening on bronze.

11

Half his days he had passed in the shadow
Of the earth: not the cold, grassy shade cast
By a pale of cypresses, by pines spread

More softly across stony hilltops; not
Warm, gray veiling of sunlight that blotted
Up his own moving shadow on the ground;

But the dark cloak of substance beyond mass,
Though heavy, flung with diurnal panache
Over his heavier head, weighed it down.

Way down at the bottom of a shaft sunk
Through the grass of sleep to deep stone he lay,
Draped in the shade cast inward by the place

All outward shadows fall upon, and on
His tongue an emerald glittered, unseen,
A green stone colder in the mouth than glass.

12

When, as if late some night of festival
The skies open, do the insides of stars
Turn slowly out? At midnight, once, he finds

Himself looking up a familiar
Street and being shown a way of water:
Bordering the calm, unsubsided flood,

Gray frame houses with darkened roofs intact,
Minding the sky of paler gray; along
The surface of gray water, the tracing

Eye's anxious questions—only these have moved.
And save where—by a window giving on
His sunken yard—someone blind makes wordless

Music while his three graceless daughters wait
In the shadows for evening, all is gray
Silence, save for his resolved organ chords.

13

He awoke. Low in the sky in August
Blown clear by a cold wind, thinned-out clusters
Of distant stars whistling through darkness struck

Out at a momentary Jupiter
Passing at night, bright visitor, among
The passages of his twinkling bazaars.

And saw strung in the Scorpion a jewel
Of unmarred garnet, the old, the reddened
But not with shed blood, nor with ripening.

And saw and read by the diamonded Harp,
By crossbow Swan aimed along the pale stream
Southward, by all the miles of undialled light,

By the mark missed, by the unstinging tail,
The moment that was: the time of this dark
Light beyond, that seemed to be light above.

14

Grayish flakes like clay are falling as if
Of the sky falling at last on Chicken
Big, now grown huge and old, examining

The falling daylight from her crowded house,
The plausible, settled-for gray, dropping
Out of its cloudy, indeterminate

Swirl, its pale precipitate vanishing
At the full bottom of its fall, too light
To have swerved, too general to pile up,

These flakes of day, in a reaction
As if of flakes of, say, fictions taking
Place *in vitro,* trembling as the flask shakes—

In vivo then? behind this mottled glass
The awakener hears the greasy rain
Collapse on unglistening streets below.

15

The bright moon offends him: he plucks it out;
He opens all the seals of touch; he hears
The whirlwinds of his breathing; then it comes:

A last waking to a trumpet of light
From warm lamps turns him over gravely toward
Her long, bare figure, Lady Evening,

Who, while he lay unwaking, rearranged
Oddments of day on a dressing table,
Lowered gentle blinds, letting the night dawn,

And thought of their sole parting, the breaking
Of day; his journeys into day's mock night;
His sojourn with lilting Miss Noctae, witch

Of windless darknesses; his presiding
Eye, and his slowly unwinding heart;
Then lay beside him as the lamps burned on.

THE SHADES

1

Even the white shade could flap a black wing
As it flew and wrapped itself up, clearing
Stark panes of upper window—glassy light
Slapped his eye from a sudden firmament.
When lowered, they yielded up pale shades thrown
By an inner light past the opaque ones
They were ghosts of—the pallor of the shades
Took more toll of his waking eye than dark.
And, when drawn, black ones made the scene they framed
Squint, his large light-gathering glass ducking
Below the edge where the flat night machine
Widened the strip of wall, bed, and undressed
Flesh into a picture. And his eyes were opened,
As in blinding light the hand's shade allows.

2

"In enigma, the eyes hide their own light
Behind owl eyes of darkling glass; we find
Dull scales hardening on vision's surface
As if the unskeptical patient hoped
Somehow to chain down the beasts of wild glare,
The lions of the light. The prognosis
Is neither here nor there," the Ophthalmage
Muttered over his speculum, tapping
On the onyx tabletop, which glistened
To him unhearing, being too wild-eyed
In the way of dark spectacles which fail
To widen the openings they cover,
Two tiny bullet holes known to be too
Narrow, punched through the yielding skin of mind.

3

Feeling their dark ones to have been darkened
By the cast shadows of men full on men,
They considered how the unsounded caves
Everywhere glistened; how in the silence
Of noon, there in the square, all the lighted
Sepulchres threw no shadows about them
Nor none within; how they were all faded
Angels of each other, met outside a
Garden's walls whereon their own shadows fell,
Within which walked the clear, transparent ones,
The pair of glass, whose shadows permitted
—Everything was permitted—light outlined
By their shining-edged forms to pass back up
To clear eyes from the green, mirroring grass.

4

Black Wolfgang and gray brother Ludwig, two
Shades of cat, pussyfoot down the long hall.
All the Crayola boys in flowery
Surplices sing out of their stalls in praise
Of paling and of darkening, the light
Diastole, the heavier return,
Joy being in their dance of contrasts, life
Hanging between earthwardness and the air.
Too much of too many colors brings mud,
Touches of pale water lead to lightness,
But all gathered by the eyes' firelight,
Whose very flickerings discern themselves
To be waltzing in the masquerade of
Degree, each denser he whirling off with
Her, his frail one, darkening in his arms.

5

Never having, like orange monarchs, claimed
Bright meadows rich with daylong, green milkweed,
Or flamed amazement over a gazer,
They mottle the walls of hell; they stand in
Fives in the unreturning *traghetto*
Or wrapped up in shades of death accosting
The fancy wanderers in their tunnel;
Unprimed for darkness cast on their eyelight
Itself, these find no shadows of shades here,
No shadows more than shadows of flesh, no
Flickering images of soul, no soul—
The body's pale nightmare of mind, faded;
The mind's drop of frightened sweat at mere thought
Of body, unglistening, chilled and dried.

6

With the light ever going, they live with
No walker in the cool of the evening,
Acknowledging light under chestnut leaves
In solemn motley genuinely flecked;
Uncheckered their dale, their evening no flung
Counterpane nor dark-knitted comforter,
Even, under which they crowd with their own
Heats and lights still clutched and minded; feeling
The first chill of autumn only in sleep,
They awaken to yellow sun ducking
Low under the shades to stretch trapezoids
Over a dark floor. And they sleep unminding
The time of afternoon, nearly before
The cold fading unrolled along the grass.

TALES TOLD OF THE FATHERS

1 THE MOMENT

In a cold glade sacred to nothing
He stood waiting, withholding his gaze
From unquestioned sky, unanswering
Grass, he later supposed, all the while
Growing unfelt beneath his bared soles.
The sky was not green although the grass
Was gray, and he felt the moment pass,
With no breath, when some ten of them might
Have come whispering through the dark brush,
Past spaces of water and beyond
Regions of erased shapes in the air,
To conduct him far away on foot
To a place not of earth, but only
Of abominations: dirt and soil,
Shit and mud mingling in wet trenches,
Where he would have stood bound and retching,
Aghast, but of course unsurprised as
Soundlessly the things were done, as then
The trembling foal dropped into a vat
Of rotten wine, the kid fell forward
Into the seething milk—but the wind
Breathed for him; the moment came and went
For the thin ten that time. He would wait.

2 THE PICTURES

His reflection in water said:
The father is light's general,
The son is but a morning star
Whose very rising into the
Failure of daylight makes the great
Case of upward fall—O see him
Bleaching out in the high morning!

His cold shadow on the rock said:
Under me, unshading, lies the
Skeleton of an Indian.
The dead. The dead are not even
Things. No odd beings. Stones and bones
Fall away to bone and stone then
To crumbling, then to part of night.

3   A CUP OF TREMBLINGS

Facing deep wine raised in the
Tilted, earthen cup, the dark
Opening into further
Dark, eyes wide, he could perceive,
Around the rim of the dark,
Breathings of the afternoon;
As, eyes shuttered, he could see
Sleep, so, opened, they would show
Him death—but now momently
In the heart of the wine, far
Away, the muses of waltz
Moved, as if seen from a height
Down a narrowing defile,
In an unshadowed meadow.

4   THE SIGN

When he saw a skull floating
On the face of the waters
With a mind of air and eyes
Of wind, it was not a sign
Of drowning generations
Themselves now drowned. It was no
Mere wonder of mirroring,
But part of the garbage of
Pain, the usual offal

Of encounter: a fallen
Top of something no choiring
Winds' melismata question,
The dark, hollow shard of a
Vessel of decreated
Clay, a cup of life emptied.

—And seeing it just at noon,
Bobbing on bright water at
The most transparent time, when
He could look back over his
Shoulder and see a clear field,
When his long, ever-vengeful
Shadow vanishes and stops,
For a moment, following:
This was most dreadful of all.

5 THE GARDEN

High on his brick cliff his garden hung
Open eastward and backed against the
Heights that hid the broad, showy deathbed
Of the sun, whose Tiepolo gestures
He read raving reviews of in the
Fiery mirrors of the west-watching
Windows set in other distant cliffs.
It was there that he muttered about
His pots of spiky dill and broad mint,
His borders of concealing privet.
Edenist of the mid-air, he gazed
At the black oily kernels of dust
Flung as if by some high sower and
Languidly fallen through the forenoon
Over the walls, mingling with his soil.
He had had to make do among smut
And fruitless grit; had lopped and pruned all

The branches of shadow and with care
Hung the leathern mock-adder among
His greens to scare grumbling doves away.
In the evening cool his dull cigar
Breathed and glowed. This was all that there was
To keep. And there was nothing to lose.

BEING ALONE IN THE FIELD

What had I fallen to? Even the field
Felt higher than I, the ghosts of its oats
Waving invisibly in the purple
Air above me and the height of my eye.

The sight of my eye lowered toward rising
Ground, the light of my sigh sown there, the cry
Of blood rising toward the spirits of wheat
Rusting their high ears, the listening dew

—All had composed themselves in the field, where
The darker air had flown and alighted,
And there was no light by which I might read
The field, much less as I had always done

Make it out through the Book of the Fair Field,
Or some such book. There was surely no light
For that. The absorbing bare field alone
Lay open like a blind eye turned upward.

I lay flat thus against the horizon
Which drew in towards the ground, as the flat night
Prepared in all directions save for that
Of height its draped, illegible deathbed.

ROTATION OF CROPS

Farmer John wandered among his fields
Feeling a tedium of the soil
Lifted by no pious following
Of oats by peas, then of peas by beans,
And then beans by orient barley,
Or even the peaceful fallowness
Yielding what little that peace can yield.
No dew pearled rough furrows with early
Seeds of shining along their low sills.

What could revolve there was not the sun.
Twilight kept shifting between evils
—Heaviness, then alleviation;
Only Sol smoldered with tedium
In the untenanted meads above,
There, where no other kinds of light grazed.
Below, no other kinds of light grew.
"And so, and so" groaned the Farmer John
And gazed at the vagueness of his grain.

But then after dark the night itself
Shifted her ground: cerements of turf
Flung back the rough darkness threshed away
From fire toward the stars' clear counterpane;
Hectares of millet, disgusting fields
Of vetch, acres of darkened corn, were
Turning in the starlight that seeded
Them all, while the sleeping Farmer gleaned
Mindfulls from outside the mills of light.

THE ZIZ

What is the Ziz?
                    It is not quite
Written how at the Beginning,
Along with the Behemoth of
Earth and the deep Leviathan,
A third was set forth (as if air
Could share a viceroy with fire,
A third only): This is the Ziz.

The Rabbi   Can we thrall him and his entailed
Aquila then   Space in our glance? And can we cast
asked: A look wide enough to draw up
A glimpse of fluttering over
The chimney-stacks, of flashing in
Huge fir-boughs, or among high crags
Sinking at dusk? How could we have
Lime or twigs or patience enough
To snare the Ziz? The Phoenix lives
Blessedly in belts of hidden
Fire, guarding us from the hurt of
Light beyond sunlight: but where is
The Ziz? A gleaming, transparent
Class, kingdom of all the winged?
Pre-existing its instances,
It covers them, it covers us
With no shadow that we can see:
But the dark of its wings tinges
What flutters in the shadows' heart.

Even more,   In their last whispered syllables
Rabbi Jonah   The muffled whatziz, the shrouded
said: Whooziz (trailing a sorrowful
Feather from beneath its cloak) tell
False tales of the Ziz: his is not

Theirs, nor he their wintry answer.
—Nor should we desire August light,
Showing a prematurely full
Sight of the Ziz entire, lest we
See and see and see our eyes out:
No: Praised be the cool, textual
Hearsay by which we beware the
Unvarying stare of the Ziz
In whose gaze curiosity
Rusts, and all quests are suspended.

At which   One day at the end of days, the
Ben-Tarnegol   General Grand Collation will
recalled: Feature the deliciously
Prepared Ziz, fragrant far beyond
Spiciness, dazzling far beyond
The poor, bland sweetness of our meals;
Faster than feasting, eternal
Past the range of our enoughness:
So, promised in time, the future
Repast; but now, only vastness
We are blind to, a birdhood
To cover the head of the sky.

COHEN ON THE TELEPHONE

Hello? Something wrong again? O hell!
—Rather darkness audible, abuzz
With nasty wings small enough to whirr
Electrically in a forest
Of noises through which no darkling bird
Squawks its response to darkness, or shrills
Its orisons toward the edge of light.
No lost or dropped angels wander here:
The ghosts of noise are only of noise.

Telephones? Well, a sage said, *they can*
Teach that what we say Here is heard There.
But, grinding away at homely bells,
We can no longer talk to Central;
The Exchanges are unmanned; the poles
Are blown down; your three minutes are up.

Instruments? They are deaf: yea, the sweet
Harp of the psalmist could never hear
Its own early arpeggios rising.
The distant ringing is not the sound
Of another's bell reduced to dry
Gasps: it is produced against your ear.
It is not Levi on the Muzak,
Fiddling tonelessly with the bright dials.
It is Ben Cole, the son of your voice,
Questioning along the deep cables,
Sad and nasal even in his yeas.

And once connected to chaos, then
What engulfs you is the babbling of
The multitude of your descendants
Who clamor for a hearing now, not
Then, begetting echoes of themselves

Even as they swarm in the light wind
That blows among jungles of wiring:
Come, come they sang, but *Abbadabba*
Now they sing; until, as if you heard
The planet's end, they are clicked away.
No dial-tone, like a patient front door
May yet open on fields of people,
Bright fields. There is no waiting for dark,
Nor will the long silence break with light.
But from near, from far, unechoing
In the black sea shell you, landsman, hold
Close against your ear, it comes, it comes:

The next voice you hear will be your own.

A SEASON IN HELLAS

You know a region higher than these crags?
A painted castle flying silly flags
Imprisons a spoiled princess, robed in fur,
Daily awaiting a dark torturer.
You know the place? O there, O there,
On fire, O my destroyer, we shall fare!

You know the valley where a thinning stream
Reflects no hopeful spires, no peaks of dream?
A ruined roadway winds down from the pass
Toward sullen sheep, gray in the withering grass,
You know the place? O there, O there,
At dawn, O my deserter, I shall stare!

You know the bed in a long-windowed room?
Night-colored curtains stir, black roses bloom;
Where moonlit harpstrings glitter like a crown
My silvery double enters and lies down.
You know the place? O there, O there,
O my lost self, we both dissolve in air!

MOUNT BLANK

for David Kalstone

*Accessible by reasonably good roads most of the year; pass
open from the North, July & August. At 1973m. a rest-
house, from which one can walk, or ride by cable car, to
the western summit. The eastern face should not be at-
tempted without a guide.*

——Until, the next morning in the sun, there
It was, framed in the window, looking like
The intense pictures of itself, which all
The night before while the ravening black
Swallowed the hills, engorged the dim vales, sucked
Up starlight through holes in the pines, and coughed
At the half-latched gate, all the night before
He lay awake, trying to remember:
Snowy veils of spume blown across the gorge;
A view shot upward dizzyingly while
The unseen ravine somehow made itself
Known, out of the picture; even the mere
Gorgeousness of depth, rock and height had dimmed.
His cold remembrances raved in the dark,
Houring after images. Midnight
Was no minimum, though: no skier whizzed
Past its momentary flatness, down one
Half parabolic dream of slope and up
Its opposite. The deadly hours which
Followed neither sank nor rose toward the day,
But merely stretched. The pictures were all wrong,
Those which came. They were pictures of pictures,
Or views of noise: postcards of roaring, as
Of mighty waters from the top of Mount
Throwdown; illuminations of the blasts
Hammering the clear tops of Mount Windows.

Or else they mirrored certain infamous
Peaks, quite as if to lead him by the head
To some mad eminence—say, the summit
Of Nayvel, to howl a loud howl like, "Down,
Be thou my Up." Or else they reflected
The ludicrous Snifflehorn rising from
His flat face on the plain bed, pictures far
Too close to themselves, and too close to him.

No, there were to be no comparisons—
Nor of the splended reals of the morning
With night's thin images, nor of the blaze
Of day with what lay banked in a black stove,
Nor of the pictured with the picturing.
For he awoke to a deluge of light,
And, rising far beyond that light in which
His eyesight gleamed, the old and the famous
Peak, preposterous—that was what he faced.
And if it had been cut out of cardboard,
Cardboard would serve. It always had: inside
Contours part jagged, part caressingly
Smooth—for even children were trained to trace
Its silhouette that they might come to know
It—there was only the unmarked flatness
Of surface fused to its depth. What he saw
Was not a picture of his seeing, nor
An image of his dimmest sleep. And, say,
That there was no cardboard (or, if there were,
A little azure hat for the mountain,
Doing no harm), say that the crookedness
Of its high tower was a beckoning,
And that it was a place to get to—still,
Cardboard is as cardboard does: biting out
Its parts of the available blue and
Masking some gummier construction taped
Behind it, emptiness and passe-partout.

And yet the vision of it hung there seemed
A vision as of something rounded, cut
Into by the wild blades of icy air,
Scooped and shaped if only by its shadows,
Troughed by a glacier and likely as not
Hacked out with caves and rock-studded across
An unseen face. And he knew a cold wind,
Then. It brought with it, as it might carry
A distant shouting among its own yells,
A blast of glimpsing from afar, a speck
Of mountaineer against the blue, plunging
Slowly from the far summit. Then the wind
Died. Frost on the glass outside gleamed under
The mounting sun, the cold snowfields stretching
Between his crying eye and that height, the
Fell beacon, gray, unsurmounted with light.

OFFICER'S QUARTERS

This room is lit by winter

And this stove, giving heat and keeping what light it has within it,

Is yet doing an act of light, even to the corner of the room

Where Captain Consciousness sits at the bare table, writing by the
    light of his own hand

Outside in the northern sky, above the frozen canal, dark specks of
    duck

Undiscernible as bird, but flying away:

Inside, the bright images and hard-edged, in the warmth, the radiance.

THE PROBLEM OF PAIN

Love is not a feeling. Love, unlike pain, is put to the test.
One does not say:
"That was not a true pain because it passed away so quickly."
WITTGENSTEIN

The problem of pain was that there was no problem.

On the torn page there were parts of a diagram, but the proof, the proof had not been ripped.

Like a madman leaning on the loudest bell-button, the Toothacher, behind the clouds outside, pressed neither in stupor nor in rage;

But the drilling bell never diffused into the dark air of silence.

The particle clinging to my eyeball remained an intruder; his visit could fructify in no gleaming pearl.

Spasms assaulted out of the dark of back: below that plain over which we have no eyes to gaze, they could have been hiding anywhere.

The flash of burning was soundless; its moment of waiting, dark; but its echo of hurt, crescendo, silenced the scoffers, the disbelieving tourists who stood at the edge of the gorge.

And the lunatic Toothacher again, after some years. We had moved to another city: he should not have known our address.

And his noise continued to remind us of nothing.

They all sounded, these penetrations, like nothing but themselves.

The one they called, half-fondly, *cramp* has a real name that rhymes with no word in any known language,

But which the calf of a leg roars out, wrenched in a sea of bedsheets.

Not like the twilight of fever,

Flooding the inner jungles with a lulling music: Wagnerian, or whitening river water, or the remembering click of wheels on rails—

Not like the shades of sorrow a kind hand drew over the afternoon
sun, down the sickroom windows, softening the edges of things
that would otherwise blur—

Nor the warming ache of strain.

Nor weariness, the final weariness shedding its wisdom over recum-
bent forms, long and lumpy beneath the blankets' shroud.

EXAMPLES

for I. A. Richards

DESCARTES' WAX

Ah yes, the wax; this piece just now unhived, now in my hand—

Honey-smelling yet, that honey yet flower-smelling, those flowers

(Say, they are purple clover, outgrowing the white)

Still remembering their houses of grass, whose green breathings

Themselves lead back into redolence, in eternal regress,

Stirred by the mind's winds; while in its house of silence,

This wax, tawnier than the honey, shines with a noble yellow,

Lion-color, golden as a beast from which strength is plucked,

A hardened blob: warmth will make it give, warmth of the near
     candle's glowing mind

Lump of cerebrum: my thumbnail lines it into two lobes which
     caresses will spread

Or curl

And then, and then anything

A waning of sameness: but from where—

Hoard of forms hidden in a high mountain cave? the sky's inexhaus-
     tible grayblue Morpheum?—

Will it take shape?

RUSSELL'S MONARCH

"The present king of France is bald";

For some years he has gone without the fiction of false hair,

Fringed with a slipped, half-glory of white, while a corollary gleam

Shines from his pate in the bright light, above a land of green,

As he stands for a moment, ivory orb and cue in either hand,

In the grand billiard-room at Monterreur,

Still suggesting some of his earlier pictures: as on the east terrace back
at Montraison

In the clear light that spoke silently of betrayals, he stood watching,

First the light itself and then, distantly, welcoming clouds.

And he sighed for the truth.

Or as in state of some kind, with much plum-colored velvet swagged
behind him,

The heavy, dripping sleeve of an abstract arm whose hand may be
pointing somewhere,

Or keeping something out of sight.

But if one is mistaken about him, finds out he has crowned nonentity
with the pinchbeck of language,

Elevating him who could not even be considered a pretender,

Then say, rather "The present king of France" is bald, is too crude an
instance;

For by the blunders by which we climb, those mistakes our handholds

Are less stark than the rocks we seek to rise above,

And these: the fullness and the curl of wigs, moving above a sea of
shoulders,

Or reposing broodily on their wooden eggs at night—

Are our additions to what is given, our patches for what is always being
taken away.

TAKING THE CASE OF THE DONKEYS (*Austin*)

Spare philosophers in a bright field stand shooting at donkeys

Across the cold distance of rocky ground on which they are not

Toward pasture, and the gray, earnest ones grazing there,

One of whom finally drops, hit by accident,

Another, by mistake; but both by an unrelenting intent that they serve
    not as beasts of burden,

But, winged with the Exemplary, as creatures of the mind's flight.

The philosophers may not love them—their deaths are so ridiculous!—

But that would be because the philosophers are exemplary as well;

Dropping their rifles to the misty ground, and slowly merging with its
    colors,

They amble toward the melted beasts and ride them solemnly

Out of our sight.

MOORE'S BEASTS

"Tame tigers growl"

Or not, as the case may be;

But some tame tigers who do not exist are ever silent of throat,

Just as they are never narrowed of eye.

Silence of paw is something else: I have been brushed by the passage
　of fiery fur

And heard soft padfall, like the slopping of something damp in the
　long hallway;

I have heard the rip and then the shredding of stretched canvas

As, patiently standing, one paw against the golden foliage of frame,

One of them came to know, after weeks of contemplation,

That a landscape of dim forests must, in fact, go.

An ounce of tears watered the carpet and his face.

I have heard them lying half asleep along the hard terraces, their
　guarded breathing.

But mostly these children of fear are seen and not heard,

Passing across open doors, slow huge heads turning dark corners,

Looking back down corridors as if—and what can one make of the
　silences of our beasts?—

Regretful: unhurried, but surely regretful.

7 + 5 = 12 (*Kant*)

I think I see why this one: two primes aimed at the all but inevitable composite

—The one which should, had we two subsidiary thumbs, have been our numberer,

A reasonable base for those airy towers untopped, paling into distances—

But, out of some gentleness, not stepped crudely upward,

Five and seven and then their sum—as if climbing were all that vertical scales were for—

Instead more warmly abstract: dipping in order to rise, but barely whispering of that,

Nor of mystery taken and pent up in hand.

Hand in hand, their *tableau vivant* never over,

They yet bow and smile, asserting a truth radiant even in daylight,

Like what lay somewhere between the given and the found,

Always golden and unspeakably glittering down in the cellars.

BREADTH. CIRCLE. DESERT.
MONARCH. MONTH. WISDOM.
(for which there are no rhymes)

> Not as *height* rises into lightness
> Nor as *length* strengthens—say, the accepting eye
> Calmed by a longing of shoreline—
> *Breadth* wields its increase over nothing, to the greater
> Glory of nothing: our unwanted dimension,
> > Yet necessary.

> What the *square* can share of its rightness
> Extends a just plainness; the sure swerve of a
> *Curve* continues beyond itself.
> But O, the old closure! *Circle* of will returning
> Inward to prison, wrenching all tangencies back,
> > Lest there be friendship

> Even in clever touchings that the
> *City* solders with pity or with desiring,
> > Or of *mountain's* unique bond with
> The fountains gushing forth from it that cry out of high
> Things. Solitariness of *Desert* ever
> > Stretches out in vain,

> Lonely *Monarch* of all who survey
> Its wearying inclusiveness, subject to
> No true attachments as a *fool's*
> To his toy tool, jingling self-image, nor object of
> Blunderings that it keeps ever breeding—*wife* of
> > Self-created strife.

Sole rondures of *day* unrolling stay
The approach of stillness, and between them and
The larger wheel of *year* appear
The lunar counterturns in cold, reflected selfhood
Of *Month,* unbound to sun but only barely out
Of phase with its rounds.

These solitaries! whether bright or
Dim, unconstellated words rain down through the
Darkness: after *youth* has burned out
His tallow truth, and *love,* which above everything must
Cling to word and body, drains, *Wisdom* remains full,
Whole, unrhymable.

Intone them then: *Breadth Circle Desert
Monarch Month Wisdom* not for whatever spell
They generate but for their mere
Inexorable syntax. The eye's movement outward
Claims its huge dominions not by kinship, nor bond
Of common ending.

KRANICH AND BACH
(A brand of piano no longer made)

Under her golden willow a golden crane
Hangs over golden water, stencilled on the
Heavy lamplit brown of the solemn upright:

Silence standing in a pool of reflection?
Or, if the brook's waters rumble darkly on,
Silence reflecting by a flow of music?

No golden harp with golden wires depends from
The vaulted branch on the shiny varnished ground,
Mirroring the ebony and ivory,

And the glint of golden from a wedding-band,
And the earnest hands of my poor father, who
With forgotten fingers played as best he could,

Muttering, or even roaring out the texts:
Erl-King strokes the boy; trout die in their now-dulled
Stream; the wan Double carries on in moonlight;

Impatience stutters on the keys; water turns
Through its rippling figures, and always the old
Man, bare amid a few tattered chords, still stands

Grinding out his music, *dyum de dum dum dum:*
"Both his feet are bare upon the frozen ground,
In his empty saucer no coin makes a sound."

Lyre-man, I would not know for years that you
Stand at the end of a journey of winter
To be followed only into its silence

As I will follow my father into his.
Dark under the closed lid, Kranich and Bach wait,
Silence standing up one-leggedly in song.

THE MUSE IN THE MONKEY TOWER   (Via dei Portoghesi)

for James Wright

American girl, within
Your room up in the tower
Above darkening houses
That squat along darkened streets,
Come to your window or his,
Because it eyes his wider
One which frames it in sunset—

Peer like a kind of day out
Of one region into all
Others, lighting up even
The farrowing street at noon
With what comes out of the dark.
Now while all the visible
Angels rest their stone trumpets

In the hot light, Olive, for
Instance, recollects her brood
Of cloudy doves, passengers
For ages beyond our own:
Ripe-eyed, she keeps all the rest,
But what will come will never
Come of the peaceable hours;

Thus Myrtle, perhaps, our old
Dear substrate, mincing to what
One might dare call her casement,
Would beam admittance to her
Shady bed and a hot fuck
Under the *tramontana:*
What was to come would not cool;

And even Laura, cooler
Than the darkest greens of her
Northwest, waiting for evening
As long as if for ever,
Aureate hair catching a
Brightness from beyond her own,
Leaping from the wider day:

No, that lady will not be
Whistled for, and the comic
Lauro from downstairs, poking
Out of his hole in the wall
Shouting for Massimo, comes
Justly rebuking the wrong
Call directed far too high.

You there who are left, Judith
Or Joan or whoever dwells
In the magic tower now,
Gaze across with eyes of sky
Into the shadowed room where
He waits for what will come and
Seize him as if with your light.

From Town and Country Matters

SONNETS FOR ROSEBLUSH

Since bed's the only world of pure idea
That history has left us; and our forms,
Glowing invisibly in darkness here,
Alone transcend the black, galactic storms,
The last two universals; to conclude
That you're unreal except when both my hands
Are clapped around your ass and lassitude
In a mad world of shadows shows us lands
That lie below Atlantis, just this side
Of sleep, is no Platonic sloppiness:
Not come to bed yet, after having died,
You're only human, and I'm somewhat less;
Until this sheet, with both of us upon it,
Tosses us essences into a sonnet.

Like the bright Ladies of the Sonneteers
Who only became real inside a poem,
You stop existing during all those years
Between the Jubilees when we're at home
In bed, at work, or play (depending on
Love's season). What you do out there by day
Is literary; walking to the john
Or getting up to shut the window's gay
Romantic fiction. Truth and circumstance
Are here and now, upon this mattress, where
(Uncross your legs while I pull down your pants)
Fabric of vision yields to skin and hair.
Nature is what we're doing; it takes art
To dream a life of which this act's a part.

I can do you and Dame Philosophy
At once, without incurring jealousy:
Inside his girl, any poor student finds
That other bodies aren't other minds.
Just so, I've learned that what it is I feel
When fitted into you's the same old real
World that my elbow on the mattress tells me
Can't lie, or change its mind, the world that quells me
When, in contracting, it can seem to know
Me in the sense I know you're here below.
I can be your pain; you are still my world.
Our mixed-up categories lie here, curled
 Not in real sympathy, but just in touch:
After too long, it gets to be too much.

Were Sade and Sacher-Masoch Jacobins
For nothing? Shoulder to shoulder, on the shelf,
Justine and *The Furred Venus* bare their sins.
One smashed the Other, the other one, the Self,
Yet both were enemies of bondage, when
That bondage was not self-imposed. Below
This row of moralists, now and again
We took our sad and learnèd pleasures, though
The usual feudal screwing might have bored
Sade, whom tight bands of passion bound to his victim
Or Masoch (when he'd made his lady lord)
Whose will wielded the thorns with which she pricked him.
Egalitarian enough for two,
Sometimes, love, I'll insist on what we'll do.

Charlus, chained to his bed at Jupien's—
No man, we're told, has ever been more free.
I don't know how this paradox extends:
My magnet hand, sliding above your knee
Toward a far stronger core, is not unwilling;
Its claim to bondage is my poor excuse.
And giving up the ghost, that sudden spilling
Is welcome death in mutual abuse.
Perhaps submission, that a height be gained
Is just like *credo ut intelligam*,
A language game, played indoors when it rained,
Until I won it, with my finger, thumb
And one free hand, trembling with love and fear
Of what determined me, yet felt so near.

There's more, dear, to this kind of paradox:
We know how supple Epimetheus
With his stiff key, unlocked Pandora's box
And pushed inside, past all the fret and fuss
Toward fluttering wings of hope: she shut him up
Thereby, and fled into a world of girls,
Giggles and curiosities. His cup
Was empty, but undrained. Just so, these curls
Around your keyhole, tiny, soft and flat
Whisper together as I stroke them now,
Plot my imprisonment—once I'm in, that's that:
I'm jailed and jilted, and your binding vow
Of liberty is snapped, here on this bed.
We screw because there's nothing to be said.

All right! We talk too much! There are degrees
Of intimacy beyond adoration:
When Diotima took on Socrates
Their lips and tongues were chained to conversation.
A clever father of a girl once told her:
'Say something interesting, and then they'll stop.'
She soon grew wise before she was much older
And left off talking once I'd climbed on top.
But language, lighting up this darkness, shows
Far more than blackest silence can the way
Our mouths can take us. A brilliant notion goes
Down into action: we are what we say,
Knowing is feeling, telling is touching, summing
Up is attacking: being true is coming.

There you are, free of mediating dress
At last, standing half-turned away from me;
For the first time my gaze's long caress
Alights on form, molds your entirety.
We'll turn again to warm, envisioning touch
Who felt through the cloth, darkly, to begin:
My eyes' light stroking can't delay too much
The finger's face-to-face of final skin.
Your image now, though, undraped and intact:
Full moon, clear of her velvet déshabille?
The destitute, cold nakedness of Fact?
Truth in her unencumbered nudity?
Venus and Truth in the old handbooks show
The same bare image you have let me know.

Now you walk toward me and the windowed moon,
Shedding the draperies that shadow lays
Over your pale entirety, which soon
Falls into parts, under the hands of praise.
Even the poor, trapped Paris could award
That bright, permitted fruit to none but you,
Had you been there, a fourth; but here, adored,
Your vying goddesses crowd round and sue—
Wise mouth, high-regnant breasts and lovely cunt—
For all that Discord gave me: shall I start
By honoring the Highest? Shall I hunt
Middle-ground? Is the Last the golden part?
Who waits to win, with a faint, blushing itch?
Just let me touch them, and I'll tell you which.

This old, carved bed where we lie garlanded
Mirrors our intertwinings; festoons smile,
Aping the forms that Grinling Gibbons hid
In wooden mockeries of green. Meanwhile,
Crowded with ghosts, its moonlit sheets lie whitely;
We twist among them and my hands evade
Remembered openings and caves politely,
Then plunging, thankfully, into your shade.
The bed's not haunted: we have brought these spooks—
Protean partners, changing at each touch—
Locked in the moist leaves of your private books,
On the stiff finger that I use to turn them.
Blame not this grand old bed for ghosts and such,
But our poor parts of wisdom that discern them.

But as we move, surrounded by an orgy
Of all our emanations, there are others
Standing about, whose grimmer dramaturgy—
Girls and their fathers, all those boys and mothers—
Menaces from a distance, far more tragic
Than a satyric sprawl amongst ourselves
And parts of old loves, mixed by harmless magic.
From photographs, from niches and from shelves
Meanwhile, commanding silently and waiting
For the poor interlude to end, their fact
Feigns the true play, for which our penetrating
Farce can only serve as an *entr' acte:*
In an unsmiling ring around us dance
The choruses of family romance.

Why drink, why touch you now? If it will be
Gin from the beginning, ending there,
For me, in the unblaming rain we see
Outside your window, filling all the air?
If, in the marvellous middle of it all,
Gin-drops of sweat come splashing down like rain
On both our bodies? If, once each, we call
The other's name as if in final pain?
Why then go through with it, when to imagine
What we shall do, what we shall be, is still
The noblest work of all, the sovereign region
Enduring, green, beyond both wish and will?
Why, naked and trembling, act out such old laws?
Because because because because because.

[1962–1972]

From The Night Mirror

THE NIGHT MIRROR

What it showed was always the same—
A vertical panel with him in it,
Being a horrible bit of movement
At the edge of knowledge, overhanging
The canyons of nightmare. And when the last
Glimpse was enough—his grandmother,
Say, with a blood-red face, rising
From her Windsor chair in the warm lamplight
To tell him something—he would scramble up,
Waiting to hear himself shrieking, and gain
The ledge of the world, his bed, lit by
The pale rectangle of window, eclipsed
By a dark shape, but a shape that moved
And saw and knew and mistook its reflection
In the tall panel on the closet door
For itself. The silver corona of moonlight
That gloried his glimpsed head was enough
To send him back into silences (choosing
Fear in those chasms below), to reject
Freedom of wakeful seeing, believing
And feeling, for peace and the bondage of horrors
Welling up only from deep within
That dark planet head, spinning beyond
The rim of the night mirror's range, huge
And cold, on the pillow's dark side.

UNDER CANCER

On the Memorial building's
Terrace the sun has been buzzing
Unbearably, all the while
The white baking happens
To the shadow of the table's
White-painted iron. It darkens,
Meaning that the sun is stronger,
That I am invisibly darkening
Too, the while I whiten.
And only after the stretching
And getting up, still sweating,
My shirt striped like an awning
Drawn on over airlessness;
After the cool shades
(As if of a long arcade
Where footsteps echo gravely)
Have devoured the light;
Only after the cold of
Plunge and shower, the pale
Scent of deodorant stick
Smelling like gin and limes,
And another stripy shirt
Can come, homing in at last,
The buzzing of having been burnt.
Only then, intimations
Of tossing, hot in the dark
Night, where all the long while
Silently, along edges,
There is flaking away.

In this short while of light
My shadow darkens without
Lengthening ever, ever.

UNDER CAPRICORN

Frozen stubble, bone
Of the summer's cornfield, stretches
Away from the concrete belt
The road tightens against
The earth's chest. It is dry
And unbelievably cold.
They are hot, though, each
For the heat of the other: their car,
Maddened by visibilities,
Scours across the country:
Their hands, trembling with touch,
Pause for a time in cloth
But a time too long. There is no
Cover for them or their car——
Curving hummock nor bare
Slumbering lap of hollow——
To contain them while their white
And chattering flesh becomes
Enclosed in its own cells
Lest perhaps the thick and
Warming tears of love
They weep into each other
Manage to bind them up
In the company of joy;
Lest, like weather and earth
Sprung into green, he spring
Inside of her to hide
His wise head in her cave
Of promises that beyond
Winter there shall come
Bright, hot moments yet.
But crowded away in their car
From the unwarming light
By which wide fields and sky
Reflect each other's emptiness,

Their bodies, sobbing at last,
Would be reclaimed by winter.

They know such weather well.
Still, unnaturally eager,
They fly on over the bony
Road, looking out (out, never
In at each other) for somewhere
Else, for somewhere other
Than the unfailing brightness
Of these dumb, hopeful fields
Whose tongues will unlock only
In the uninventive course
Of season (like a sick
Joke about fulfillment)
Finally succeeding season.

AT THE NEW YEAR

Every single instant begins another new year;
    Sunlight flashing on water, or plunging into a clearing
In quiet woods announces; the hovering gull proclaims
    Even in wide midsummer a point of turning: and fading
Late winter daylight close behind the huddled backs
    Of houses close to the edge of town flares up and shatters
As well as any screeching ram's horn can, wheel
    Unbroken, uncomprehended continuity,
Making a starting point of a moment along the way,
    Spinning the year about one day's pivot of change.
But if there is to be a high moment of turning
    When a great, autumnal page, say, takes up its curved
Flight in memory's spaces, and with a final sigh,
    As of every door in the world shutting at once, subsides
Into the bed of its fellows; if there is to be
    A time of tallyir g, recounting and rereading
Illuminated annal , crowded with black and white
    And here and there a capital flaring with silver and bright
Blue, then let it come at a time like this, not at winter's
    Night, when a few dead leaves crusted with frost lie
  shivering
On our doorsteps to be counted, or when our moments of
  coldness
    Rise up to chill us again. But let us say at a golden
Moment just on the edge of harvesting, "Yes. Now."
    Times of counting are times of remembering; here amidst
  showers
Of shiny fruits, both the sweet and the bitter-tasting results,
    The honey of promises gleams on apples that turn to mud
In our innermost of mouths, we can sit facing westward
    Toward imminent rich tents, telling and remembering.

Not like merchants with pursed hearts, counting in dearth and dark-
ness,
    But as when from a shining eminence, someone walking starts
At the sudden view of imperturbable blue on one hand
    And wide green fields on the other. Not at the reddening sands
Behind, nor yet at the blind gleam, ahead, of something
    Golden, looking at such a distance and in such sunlight,
Like something given—so, at this time, our counting begins,
    Whirling all its syllables into the circling wind
That plays about our faces with a force between a blow's
    And a caress', like the strength of a blessing, as we go
Quietly on with what we shall be doing, and sing
    Thanks for being enabled, again, to begin this instant.

THE BIRD

from the Yiddish of Moishe Leib Halpern

Well, this bird comes, and under his wing is a crutch,
And he asks why I keep my door on the latch;
So I tell him that right outside the gate
Many robbers watch and wait
To get at the hidden bit of cheese,
Under my ass, behind my knees.

Then through the keyhole and the crack in the jamb
The bird bawls out he's my brother Sam,
And tells me I'll never begin to believe
How sorely he was made to grieve
On shipboard, where he had to ride
Out on deck, he says, from the other side.

So I get a whiff of what's in the air,
And leave the bird just standing there.
Meanwhile—because one never knows,
I mean—I'm keeping on my toes,
Further pushing my bit of cheese
Under my ass and toward my knees.

The bird bends his wing to shade his eyes
—Just like my brother Sam—and cries,
Through the keyhole, that *his* luck should shine
Maybe so blindingly as mine,
Because, he says, he's seen my bit
Of cheese, and he'll crack my skull for it.

It's not so nice here anymore.
So I wiggle slowly towards the door,
Holding my chair and that bit of cheese
Under my ass, behind my knees,
Quietly. But then as if I care,

I ask him whether it's cold out there.

They are frozen totally,
Both his poor ears, he answers me,
Declaring with a frightful moan
That, while he lay asleep alone
He ate up his leg—the one he's lost.
If I let him in, I can hear the rest.

When I hear the words "ate up", you can bet
That I'm terrified; I almost forget
To guard my bit of hidden cheese
Under my ass there, behind my knees.
But I reach below and, yes, it's still here,
So I haven't the slightest thing to fear.

Then I move that we should try a bout
Of waiting, to see which first gives out,
His patience, there, behind the door,
Or mine, in my own house. And more
And more I feel it's funny, what
A lot of patience I have got.

And that's the way it's stayed, although
That was some seven years ago.
I still call out "Hi, there!" through the door.
He screams back " 'Lo there" as before.
"Let me out" I plead, "don't be a louse"
And he answers, "Let me in the house".

But I know what he wants. So I bide
My time and let him wait outside.
He enquires about the bit of cheese
Under my ass, behind my knees;
Scared, I reach down, but, yes, it's still here.
I haven't the slightest thing to fear.

THE WILL

from the Yiddish of Moishe Leib Halpern

Now this is how I did myself in:
No sooner did the sun begin
To shine, when I was up and away,
Gathering goat-shit for my tune
—The one I wrote just yesterday
About the moonlight and the moon—
And then I put with these also
Some poems from my portfolio
In re the bible's sanctity
(Just thinking of them sickens me)
And these I wrapped up in my rag
Of an old coat, packed up like a bag,
After which, I took the whole shebang
Put up a nail, and let it hang
Outside my window, on a tray.
Adults and children passed my way
And asked what that mess up there could be,
So I answered them, on bended knee:
These are all my years; I think
They went all rotten with infection
By wisdom, and its ancient stink,
From my precious book collection.
But when my son, the little boy,
(In my sea of sorrow and cup of joy
He's just turned four) strained his eyes to see
Those summits of sublimity,
Well—I put him on my knee
And spake thus: Harken thou to me,
My son and heir, I swear that, just
As none disturb the dead in their rest,
So, when you have finally grown,
I'll leave you thoroughly alone.
Want to be a loan-shark, a bagel-lifter?

Be one, my child.
Want to murder, set fires, or be a grifter?
Be one, my child.
Want to change off girls with the speed that those
Same girls keep changing their own clothes?
Change away, my child.
But one thing, child, I have to say:
If once ambition leads you to try
To make some kind of big display
Of yourself with what's hanging up there in the sky;
If you dare (but may that time not come soon!)
To write about moonlight and the moon,
Or some poem of the bible, poisoning the world,
Then, my dear,
If I'm worth something then by way of any
Money, so much as a single penny,
I'll make my will, leaving everything
To my *Landsman,* the future Polish King.
Though we've both stopped calling each other "thou",
I'll chop up, like a miser shredding
Cake for beggars at a wedding,
All the ties that yet bind us now.
Poppa-chopper   Son-schmon
And so   help me   God in Heaven
This
Will
Be
Done.

LETTER TO JORGE LUIS BORGES:
APROPOS OF THE GOLEM

I've never been to Prague, and the last time
That I was there its stones sang in the rain;
The river dreamed them and that dream lay plain
Upon its surface, shallow and sublime.

The residues of years of dream remained
Solidified in structures on each bank;
Other dreams than of Prague and Raining sank
Under dark water as their memory waned.

And far beneath the surface of reflection
Lay a deep dream that was not Prague, but of it,
Of silent light from the gray sky above it,
The river running in some dreamed direction.

O Borges, I remember this too clearly—
Staring at paper now, having translated
Your poem of Prague, my flood of ink abated—
To have recalled it from my last trip, merely.

Three mythical cronies my great-grandfather
Was known to speak of nurture dark designs
Against my childhood: from between the lines
Of what was told me of them, I infer

How Haschele Bizensis, Chaim Pip,
The Bab Menucha and his friends, conspire
Over old pipes; sparks in a beard catch fire,
The smoke grows heavier with each slow sip . . .

I scream and wake from sleep into a room
I only remember now in dreams; my mother

Calms me with tales of Prague back in another
Time. All I remember is a tomb

Near what was called the Old-New Synagogue;
Under a baroque stone whose urn and column
Emerge in the first dawn lies, dead and solemn,
My ancestor, the Rabbi Loew of Prague.

He made The Golem (which means "embryo,"
"Potential person," much more than "machine")
And quickened him with a Name that has been
Hidden behind all names that one could know.

We have our family secrets: how the creature
Tried for the Rabbi's daughter, upped her dress
Till nacreous and bushy nakedness
Shone in the moonlight; groped; but failed to reach her—

How once, when heat throbbed in the August skies
And children were playing hide-and-seek, the Golem
Trailed the one who was It, and nearly stole him
Before the shadows rang with all their cries.

But was he circumcised? What glimmerings rose
In his thick face at evening? Were they sham?
Did he and nine men make a quorum? I am
Not, alas, at liberty to disclose.

(But how he saved the Jews of Prague is told
In a late story—from a Polish source?—
Not to be taken seriously, of course,
No more than one about the Emperor's gold.)

These tales jostle each other in their corner
At the eye's edge, skirting the light of day
(The Bab Menucha lurks not far away,

As if around a grave, like a paid mourner).

Too dumb to live, he could not touch, but muddy:
Lest the virgin Sabbath be desecrated,
The rabbi spoke. It was deanimated;
Half-baked ceramic moldered in his study . . .

Save for the Fire of process, elements
Mix sadly: Mud is born of Water and Earth;
Air knows Water—a bubble comes to birth;
Earth and Air—nothing that makes any sense.

But bubble, mud and that incoherent third,
When animated by the Meta-Name
That is no mere breath of air itself, became
The myth whose footsteps we just overheard

Together, shuffling down a hallway, Borges,
Toward its own decreation, dull and lonely,
Lost in the meager world of one and only
One Golem, but so many Johns and Jorges.

GRANNY SMITH

Deep, fallen azure she flashes,
Of the grass sky beneath our feet
Untoppled yet—the greeny one,
Waiting among the usual
Fruits of our life. And why I had
Not thought to find her here among
Apples of the earth and sun, the
Bright Americans fallen or
Plucked, was: why, freshening ever
On her fable of tree, she fell
To harvest merely; why she turned
Skull-color as the dark witch dipped
Her into something bubbling; why
She dropped, green levin, to her grave
From Newton's skyward tree; why pierced
Marbles of eyes roll up in sleep,
Thin-lidded, toward the patient dark.

HIS MASTER'S VOICE

1 Along the golden track
   Of Sunday afternoon light
   A triumph of motes, making
   Their grave, slantward descent,
   Rides down through pointed arches
   And tracery, through the screen
   Of stretched cloth, with a hint
   Of loudspeaker's metal lip
   Glistering through it. Far
   Down into the radio,
   They glide past shadowed regions
   Where time eats light. The sound
   Of Woglinde's final sighs
   Dies among unseen
   High, glimmering rocks, to linger
   Among the bits of brightness
   In the dusty caravan
   Streaming in from the window.

   A child plays with some chips,
   Red, blue and gold on a sea
   Of Chinese carpet. Hans Sachs
   Hammers and sings; the lonely
   English horn in a soundless
   Distance hovers and lasts
   In a wounded lingering.
   Plangent suspensions endure,
   Forever locked in the dying
   Light of midafternoon.

2 Quietly snorting and rasping,
   Making domestic static,
   The diligent, round head
   Of the faithful phonograph,
   Digging a shining eyetooth

Into its homing pathway's
Unnatural, parallel spiral,
Moves toward a central cave
Of silence, where there is only
Panting of breath, the whirring
Of wide worlds turning around,
All forward motion ended.
This is the song that song
Sinks into when it dies;
Crackling of no flame, crunching
Of no particular paper,
That was and will be, whenever
Another gem, intoned
Over the oom-pah-pah thinly
Starts up, and the resonant eye
Watches us while it works.
Cave canem: "Beware:
I may sing," whispers a distant
Continuing, whirling wind.

3   Swallowed by noisy midnight,
Lamp-pierced and fraught with clamoring
Presences guarding their silence,
How many voices have darkened?
——An inaudible hiss of tape,
The whispering of revision;
A pot of green leaves falling
Against white mirroring tile.
It claims an entrance, like light.
The soprano goes into her trill.
The wind gasps for breath outside,
Making the window shake
Its mortal frame, and the slatted
Blind yield a hurried rattle,
Masking my left-handed riffle
Of pages, the scratch of my pen.

ADAM'S TASK

> *And Adam gave names to all cattle, and*
> *to the fowl of the air, and to every*
> *beast of the field . . .* GEN. 2:20

Thou, paw-paw-paw; thou, glurd; thou, spotted
  Glurd; thou, whitestap, lurching through
The high-grown brush; thou, pliant-footed,
  Implex; thou, awagabu.

Every burrower, each flier
  Came for the name he had to give:
Gay, first work, ever to be prior,
  Not yet sunk to primitive.

Thou, verdle; thou, McFleery's pomma;
  Thou; thou; thou—three types of grawl;
Thou, flisket; thou, kabasch; thou, comma-
  Eared mashawk; thou, all; thou, all.

Were, in a fire of becoming,
  Laboring to be burned away,
Then work, half-measuring, half-humming,
  Would be as serious as play.

Thou, pambler; thou, rivarn; thou, greater
  Wherret, and thou, lesser one;
Thou, sproal; thou, zant; thou, lily-eater.
  Naming's over. Day is done.

From Visions from the Ramble

PROEM: A NEW LEAF

Manhattan, this hospital,
Black and terminal, throbs
Tonight in hot July
Shadowed by high night-lights,
Under sedation, beneath
Unpeeled sheets of sleep.
Breathing itself is unrestful,
Being, accomplishment
Enough, as we two sit
On the grass along the river.

"*This lawn for passive use
Only,*" the dark sign (foolishly
Invisible when the action,
Whatever it is, will happen)
Reads, some yards behind us.
We stare across, half-blindly,
At the famous lights along
The transhudsonian shore.
Off in the one direction
Left for pictures, the west
We have just before invented
On a dark bed (nearly setting,
Ourselves, to sleep) is dark;
All the final promises
That vanish there, just after
The sun's last smudges flash
Down behind clouds, are gone.
Our eyelids gently fall
Like blinds across disturbing,
Impatient visions that hurl
Themselves unfeelingly
At the wide panes of sleep.

The night around us oozes
Black realities, soon
To dry, too, into a past
Stickiness of fact.
Under exploring touch
Her fingers have discovered
A band-aid, shockingly white
In the reflected shining
Of lights from near the river,
Stuck across a thin
Layer of scab on my shoulder
Formed a few hours ago.

"Tear, Muse, this blinding bandage
From the heart's eye that your hand
And mouth alone have opened!"
She laughs, and, leaning over,
Rips off the strip of whiteness,
Kisses the place, and sighs.
A quiet tearing of paper
Is like a sigh, as, shaking
With hope now, I unfasten
What has been bound and clasped
And rip away a last
Unfilled first page, a white
Liar in its silence.

Frowning in scorn, or smiling
She stands and breathes behind me.

WAITING

The air grew hushed at the Flushing Meadows Fair grounds;
   purple
Residues of sunset vanished in the west; we crowded about
The largest water to watch the illuminations. Pale
Feathers of fountain thrust upwards; from beyond the Lagoon
   of Nations
Something roared and "Boys and Girls Together" beeped out
From orange carts behind the watchers on the water.
They waited to see what would happen to the fountains. Alf
   and Ralph
Got lost in the crowd and had to be searched for. Suddenly

A hissing and unseen serpent arose behind the blocks of
Red brick buildings on Eliot Square, hushed by the fleece
Of evening heat, its high trajectory lifting it
Above the Common into the black and boundless sky.
In the gleam of neon epistemologists, talking about
Nextness, moved out off the sidewalk, and craned their necks,
   just as

Sparklers crackled coolly in the moist dark garden.
Children stood in a ring with bits of punk, peering
Over the glint of magnesium for glimpses of each other's faces;
But just in time to frighten the four-year-old, from beyond

The gray stadium was hushed as the stone benches grew
Colder and the unpromising western sky was streaked
With smoke, and on the playing-field below workmen
Adjusted the display-pieces. She shivered and drew the black
Cardigan over her shoulders. Then, as if by accident,

A shattering flare of metals fell out over the dark
Lake, and cardboard shells of rockets, blackened and twisted,

Lay on the hard-packed, squeaky sand: fierce, concupiscent
Green of copper, ferrous wrath of red and, always
Burning above, the blinding pure white, color of flares,
Still glittered on in combined traces of after-image.
A cry shot up from the clump of shadows by the shore
And Mr. Ellis came running toward us, his hand rather burned,
But stopped and turned to watch as, finally, over the lake

The string of Chinese crackers gave up its family
Of ghosts like an accelerating motor, on the Long
Branch sidewalk, painted bright buff by the sinking sun.
A train whistled in the west toward distant Elberon,
Grass-green Elberon. A staid, inglorious Fourth
Sank into seashore night. Whisked out of the city,
The children lay on the roaring strand, while overhead
All that long summer the Von Hindenburg seemed to be
    hanging
Above the beaches: we Jews pointed into the glaring
Sunlight, up at the long, gray beswastikaed bobbin
While Europe unravelled behind it. But there, amid long lawns,
Fixed to the pivotal green turf of unwinding summer,
I stood still and heard the Fourths of July echo contingently
In the fading, brighter part of the early summer sky,
Waiting for life to explode in the next golden moment,
Waiting for cadence of waiting itself to come to light,
Cracking and bursting, and flaring up into significance.

FIREWORKS

Fire is worst, and fires of artifice thirst after more than
      Water does and consume
More than the world: the night within which the world
   Turns more brightly than we can even
     Guess burns out, while tears in a black
     Retina spurn hope of repair and
       Flare into smoky whisps.

Whispered desire for firing darkness with history, fleeing
      Lights that are strung along
Mirroring darkened waters, hissing itself
   Upward, dying in aspiration,
     Quenched in night; declaring themselves,
     Candles burn down, rockets burn up in
      Moments they will outlive.

No light can outlast darkness. But light
Is all we have to live by. Fire plays over creation
     But fireworks must do more
     Than remind. Out of the earth's heart
     Flaming salts fly upward into
     Pieces of darkness and spark,
    Silence of spaces that trusting, following
     Faces expect them to die in.

      High in that night
    The end comes in a cottony silence,
And then the painful crack begotten of all the unquietness
   Yet to be: a death too much like life.
O! like white needles in the mind's dark forests, thrust
     Up against the ear-drummed brain
     O see, O hear the rocket die!
    (Whorls and realms of light leap out, leap
Upward to color, to traces of shape, to life)

Darkness was first
And fire followed in violet, white and
Astonishments of orange, shot at the rim of emerging time,
Widening, as still it is: around
The full moon, high above this wide pavilion, hangs
An interior unpierced
Until the bunched homunculus
Head of one high-arching squib rakes
Down at the sphere, penetrates and escapes inside

The moon,
To the light that bleaches its fire
With the inaudible big bang,
The sudden thudding of shock when created
Pain, reflected in rings of thunder
Becomes an eternal remembrance.

We who have been burned, we who have watched
The sights of firing life, still celebrate
Fire with fire. Bright times
Are remembered in heightened nights
For benched spectators, awaiting streaks of light
Above the grandstand, in the park
In the darkness of wild July. When the past
Burst, erupting into event, the flames
Came hard upon
The explosion, but burnings of celebration
Flare up before the crash. The cranium
Of the world's darkened bowl seems now to crack.

We who have returned, guarding our hearts
From burning memory will not again become
Children bewildered. Wild eyes
Are forgotten, and frightening lights
Are quenched in blanketing darkness. Sheets of fire
And screaming whitenesses of dream

Are redeemed from fear of life by the black
Night of generation itself, by flights
        Of upward love
    Into your most interior hollows, O my
Sole light, my muse, my mind's uranium
    In whose star-pierced urn all my ashes die!

        For half of life
    Nights came so that I might burn
    Like a Roman candle, high inside
        The blacknesses of summer.
    Then there were fireworks. Flesh
        Learns of its half
    Of death from the mind's flashbulb white
        Coming into being, seeing
Something that must come of all this burning,
All this becoming something other than darkness.

THE NINTH OF JULY

In 1939 the skylark had nothing to say to me
As the June sunset splashed rose light on the broad sidewalks
And prophesied no war after the end of that August;
Only, midway between playing ball in Manhattan and Poland
I turned in my sleep on Long Island, groped in the dark of
    July,
And found my pillow at last down at the foot of my bed.
Through the window near her bed, brakes gasped on
    Avenue B
In 1952; her blonde crotch shadowed and silent
Lay half-covered by light, while the iced tea grew warm,
Till the last hollow crust of icecube cracked to its death in the
    glass.
The tea was hot on the cold hilltop in the moonlight

While a buck thrashed through the gray ghosts of burnt-out
trees
And Thomas whispered of the S.S. from inside his sleeping-bag.
Someone else told a tale of the man who was cured of a hurt by
the bears.
The bathtub drain in the Old Elberon house gucked and
snorted
When the shadows of graying maples fell across the lawn:
The brown teddybear was a mild comfort because of his silence,
And I gazed at the porthole ring made by the windowshade
String, hanging silently, seeing a head and shoulders emerge
From the burning *Morro Castle* I'd seen that afternoon.
The rock cried out "I'm burning, too" as the drying heat
Entered its phase of noon over the steep concrete
Walls along Denver's excuse for a river: we read of remote
Bermudas, and gleaming Neal spat out over the parapet.
In the evening in Deal my b.b. rifle shattered a milkbottle
While the rhododendrons burned in the fading light. The tiny
Shot-sized hole in the bathhouse revealed the identical twats
Of the twins from over the hill. From over the hill on the other
Side of the lake a dark cloud turretted over the sunset;
Another lake sank to darkness on the other side of the hill,
Lake echoing lake in diminishing pools of reflection.
A trumpet blew Taps. While the drummer's foot boomed on
the grandstand
The furriers' wives by the pool seemed to ignore the accordion
Playing "Long Ago and Far Away." None of the alewives
Rose to our nightcrawlers, wiggling on the other side of the
mirror.
She was furrier under the darkness of all the blanketing heat
Than I'd thought to find her, and the bathroom mirror flashed
White with the gleam of a car on seventy-second street.
We lay there just having died; the two of us, vision and flesh,
Contraction and dream, came apart, while the fan on the
windowsill
Blew a thin breeze of self between maker and muse, dividing

Fusing of firework, love's old explosion and outburst of voice.

This is the time most real: for unreeling time there are no
Moments, there are no points, but only the lines of memory
Streaking across the black film of the mind's night.
But here in the darkness between two great explosions of light,
Midway between the fourth of July and the fourteenth,
Suspended somewhere in summer between the ceremonies
Remembered from childhood and the historical conflagrations
Imagined in sad, learned youth—somewhere there always hangs
The American moment.
                              Burning, restless, between the deed
And the dream is the life remembered: the sparks of Concord
   were mine
As I lit a cherry-bomb once in a glow of myth
And hurled it over the hedge. The complexities of the Terror
Were mine as my poring eyes got burned in the fury of Europe
Discovered in nineteen forty-two. On the ninth of July
I have been most alive; world and I, in making each other
As always, make fewer mistakes.
                              The gibbous, historical moon
Records our nights with an eye neither narrowed against the
   brightness
Of nature, nor widened with awe at the clouds of the life of the
   mind.
Crescent and full, knowledge and touch commingled here
On this dark bed, window flung wide to the cry of the city
   night,
We lie still, making the poem of the world that emerges from
   shadows.

Doing and then having done is having ruled and commanded
A world, a self, a poem, a heartbeat in the moonlight.

To imagine a language means to imagine a form of life.

HUMMING

O summer, summer! somewhere a seventeenth season of heat
Is always exploding in roses; and broods of impulse, feeding
No more on their stored winters, released into later stages
Of being, buzzing, emerge from most of their lives' graves.

These nymphs the winter would perpetuate, secure
In their twigs, but the crash of thundering summer over the
    full
Cornfields has plucked from the ground the passionate cicadas,
Free to breed for a week in the maple branches, shaded
From the wide, white sunlight exhausting the best of their
    lives, to die
Suddenly, as when the sunlight baked on the singing highway
Is cut by the broad blade of shadow from the planting
Of forty yards of trees at a crossroads perhaps.
Sidewalks in the cool glade of sundown are strewn with shells,
Skulls of the dead nymphs, husks of what are not really selves,
Crunched underfoot, like piles of every dead July
Before a seventeenth summer.
                              Emerging creatures, surprised
By suddenness of growth cry out as do these bugs
With a humming that sounds to outlive the whole of the long
    summer.
It never does. Our overhearing hearts are never inured
To the drone of such a demanding band of musicians, whose
    furied
Continuous buzzing drills into our lives, agape
With a pressure that lies somewhere between persuasion and
    pain.
Agape. Like a rose unwormed yet, without having tasted of
    August
Love, I once in my seventeenth summer exposed all the forests
Of my mouth to the trill of the tireless boring insect, the sweat

Wrinkling the leather of the dentist's chair, defenceless
Against the invasion of pain in the secret places of budding
Eros; the whirring of other summers' eventual flourishing
Deferred to the eternal burr that sounded from somewhere
    inside me
And that I believed in my seventeenth summer could never die.
Could pain, finally, like noise, become the condition of life?
Like noises of whitening water roaring into silence,
Always, thus never?
                    The humming of human time is loud
And crowded with single, unbearable voices, that, hour by
    hour,
Blend more into timeless buzzing: the lightning mordent of
    high-
Tension wires strung skyward across hot green fields; sixty-
    cycle
Hum in the bloodstream of music in crowded, unscreened
    rooms,
The language of varying tone and the scream of song
    confusing
Its steadying drone; the jammed car horn heard from
    stories up
And blocks away, while the slowly-dropping summer sun
Lowers a reddening yolk into its cup in New Jersey.
Even the maddened humming, wordless, always wordless,
We do ourselves, that is never an act of speech, like denying,
Blaming or pledging or lying, nor the raising of voice to
    heights
That singing is: this is the business of being. To have heard
These undying cicadas, immortal while yet they live, is to burn
For a time in the moment itself. As the hot convertible,
Humming along the black macadam we all are, disturbs
The avenued peace of trees at the side of the road, the sudden
Noise of a horde of cicadas overcomes the surrounding summer
With a sound louder than life. Then, as our car emerges
From the singing glade into dead, white sun, the silence turns

On like a flipped switch, with a sharp crack of nothing,
Beginning the end of the humming, the humming, the end
  of the humming,
The end of remembering happening somewhere ahead in
  the dust.

THE NINTH OF AB

August is flat and still, with ever-thickening green
  Leaves, clipped in their richness; hoarse sighs in the grass,
    Moments of mowing, mark out the lengthening summer.
      The ground
We children play on, and toward which maples tumble their
  seed
  Reaches beneath us all, back to the sweltering City:
    Only here can it never seem yet a time to be sad in.
Only the baking concrete, the softening asphalt, the wail
  Of wall and rampart made to languish together in wild
    Heat can know of the suffering of summer. But here, or
      in woods
Fringing a pond in Pennsylvania, where dull-red newts
  The color of coals glow on the mossy rocks, the nights
    Are starry, full of promise of something beyond them,
      north
Of the north star, south of the warm dry wind, or east of the
    sea.
  There are no cities for now. Even in the time of songs
    Of lamenting for fallen cities, this spectacular sunset
Over the ninth hole of the golf-course of the hotel
  Should lead to no unusual evening, and the tall
    Poplars a mile away, eventually fading to total
Purple of fairway and sky and sea, should reman unlit
  By flaring of urban gloom. But here in this room, when the
    last

Touches of red in the sky have sunk, these few men,
lumped
Toward the end away from the windows, some with bleachy
white
Handkerchiefs comically knotted at each corner, worn
In place of black skullcaps, read what was wailed at a wall
In the most ruined of cities. Only the City is missing.
Behold their sitting down and their rising up. I am their
music,
(Music of half-comprehended Hebrew, and the muddied
Chaos of *Lamentations*)

The City, a girl with the curse,
Unclean, hangs on in her wisdom, her filthiness in her skirts,
Gray soot caked on the fringes of buildings, already scarred
With wearing. North, north of here, I know, though, that she
waits
For my return at the end of August across the wide
River, on a slow ferry, crawling toward the walls
Of high Manhattan's westward face, her concrete cliffs
Micaed with sunset's prophecies of stars, her hardened clay
Preserved, her gold undimmed, her prewar streets
uncluttered.
But here in this hot, hushed room I sit perspiring
Among the intonations of old tropes of despair;
Already, dark in my heart's dank corners, grow alien
spores;
These drops of sweat, tears for Tammuz; these restless
fidgetings,
Ritual turnings northward, away from here where fractured
And gutted walls seem still afire in history's forests,
Toward her, the City who claims me after each summer is over.
Returning is sweet and somehow embarrassing and awful,
But I shall be grateful to burn again in her twilight oven.

Meanwhile the cooling ground down toward the roots of the
grass

Heightens the katydids' scherzo. The men disperse in a grove
    Of spruces, while from the distant water-hazard, grunts
Of frogs resume their hold on the late-arriving night,
    And the just-defunct chants, never perfunctory, but not
    Immediate, have vanished into the familiar unknown.
When the days are prolonged, and every vision fails to blaze
    Up into final truth, when memories merely blur
    A sweated lens for a moment, night is enough of a blessing
And enough of a fulfillment. See! the three canonical stars
    Affirm what is always beyond danger of being disturbed
    By force of will or neglect, returning and unstoppable.

SUNDAY EVENINGS

All this indigo, nonviolent light will triumph.

Uneven shadows have fallen out of the darkness that waits,
Continuously created there, as in the whiteness
Of the kitchen two rooms away, icecubes are being made
With a humming of generation. Whether, earlier, it had been
Fine, with sunlight infusing the hints of ice incipient
In the blue air, with promises of gleaming winters
Already trumpeting through the blood and singing *"l'Avenir!"*
Unheard, but pounding somewhere within the inner ear,
Or whether the delaying rains and the two-day-old
Grayness of sky, grayness of generality, had
Spoiled the earlier day for being outside an apartment,
Outside a self—no matter. With night unfolding now
In every corner wherever walls meet or dust collects,
What has just been is obscured. The trickle of time and loss
Condenses along the outsides of things: this icy glass
Sweats drops of terror not its own; this room diffuses
Tiny patches of light through its half-shaded windows
Into the winking, myriad galaxies of all
New York on clear October nights—bits of a brightness

It has not, let alone can give; this world inside
These walls, condensing on the outside of my mind,
Has corners and darkenings quite unimaginable,
But visible as Presences in gray and purple light
At this time of day, of week, of year, of life, of time.
Even the usual consolations of Sunday become
A part of all its general threat: symphonic music
On heavy afternoons; the steam-heat, blanketing
A brown couch and a bridge-lamp and dark bookshelves;
No need for a meal, and too much newspaper to be read;
Rooms around this one, full of what is still undone
And what may never be; the glimpses out at tiny,
Unwise revelations of light, from rooms as high up as this,
Several blocks away. And to put an end to the near-
Darkness would hurt too much—a senseless, widening light
From an unfrosted lamp would do it.
                                        But then what?
Why, blinking. Then numbing to the icy fire of incandescence,
Lidded blinds lowering over the windows that overlook
Darknesses of the Park, this room being all the light
In the world now. And then, perhaps, Sunday will have been
   over.

But then what? Oh yes, once, perhaps, in a month of Sundays,
The exciting stars against a clear, cold, black sky
Shone down like promising, wise and truthful splinters of
   mirror.
We saw that the light was good, and meteored across
The starlight of high Manhattan to ordered arrangements of
   taxis
And blocks of apartments, and parties of frosty eyes like wide,
Entire mirrors, reflecting in joy the twinkling, burning
High overhead at the end of some windy afternoon.

But then what? The next week was full of itself, and ended,
Inevitable, in the darkening late afternoon, indoors,

On Sunday. Ended? Or was it merely the new week's beginning
Come to a bad end? No matter. Whatever ends up like this—
The day, week, year; the life; the time—can't be worth much.
On Sunday afternoons, one can have followed the blackening
Water of the river from eyes along the Drive
And then climbed up a concrete hill to one's own walls
And quietly opened a vein. *"It would be no crime in me*
To divert the Nile or Danube from its course, were I able
To effect such purposes. Where then is the crime
Of turning a few ounces of blood from their natural channel?"
Or the crime of emptying this late-afternoon room
Of all its indigo, not by the light of common
Illumination, but by a long pouring of darkness?
Yes, if it is permitted, everything is. So let it
Be. And let it be night now, at very long last,
A night outside the cycle of light and dark and Sunday,
A night in despite of fiery life, or icy time
That starts its chilling-out of the heart each week at five
Or five-thirty or so on Sunday, when the big, enlightening
    myths
Have sunk beyond the river and we are alone in the dark.

HELICON

Allen said, *I am searching for the true cadence.* Gray
Stony light had flashed over Morningside Drive since noon,
Mixing high in the east with a gray smoky darkness,
Blackened steel trusses of Hell-Gate faintly etched into it,
Gray visionary gleam, revealing the clarity of
Harlem's grid, like a glimpse of a future city below:
When the fat of the land shall have fallen into the dripping
    pan,
The grill will still be stuck with brown crusts, clinging to
Its bars, and neither in the fire nor out of it.
So is it coming about. But in my unguessing days

Allen said, *They still give you five dollars a pint at St. Luke's,*
No kickback to the interne, either; and I leaned out
Over the parapet and dug my heel in the hard,
Unyielding concrete below, and kicked again, and missed
The feeling of turf with water oozing its way to the top
Or of hard sand, making way for life. And was afraid,
Not for the opening of vessels designed to keep
Their rich dark cargo from the air, but for the kind
Of life that led from this oldest of initiations
Ending in homelessness, despondency and madness,
And for the moment itself when I should enter through
Those dirty-gray stone portals into the hospital
Named for the Greek doctor, abandoning all hope
Of home or of self-help. The heights of Morningside
Sloped downward, to the north, under the iron line
The subway holds to above it, refusing to descend
Under the crashing street. St. John the Divine's gray bulk
Posed, in its parody of history, just in the south.
Dry in the mouth and tired after a night of love
I followed my wild-eyed guide into the darkening door.

Inquiries and directions. Many dim rooms, and the shades
Of patient ghosts in the wards, caught in the privileged
Glimpses that the hurrying visitor always gets;
Turnings; errors; wanderings; while Allen chattered on:
I mean someday to cry out against the cities, but first
I must find the true cadence. We finally emerged
Into a dismal chamber, bare and dusty, where, suddenly,
Sunlight broke over a brown prospect of whirling clouds
And deepening smoke to plummet down, down to the depths
Of the darknesses, where, recessed in a tiny glory of light
A barely-visible man made his way in a boat
Along an amber chasm closing in smoke above him—
Two huge paintings by Thomas Cole opened, like airshaft
Windows, on darkening hearts, there by the blood bank.
We waited then and the dead hospital-white of the cots

Blinded my eyes for a while, and filled my ears with the silence
Of blanketing rushes of blood. Papers and signatures. Waiting;
And then being led by the hand into a corner across
The narrow room from Allen. We both lay down in the
    whiteness.
The needle struck. There was no pain, and as Allen waved,
I turned to the bubbling fountain, welling down redly beside
    me
And vanishing into the plasma bottle. My life drained of
    richness
As the light outside seemed to darken.

                                        Darker and milder the stream
Of blood was than the flashing, foaming spray I remembered
Just then, when, the summer before, with some simple souls
    who knew
Not Allen, I'd helped to fill Columbia's public fountains
With some powdered detergent and concentrated essence of
    grape,
Having discovered the circulation of water between them
To be a closed system. The sun of an August morning fired
Resplendently overhead; maiden teachers of English
From schools in the south were moving whitely from class to
    class
When the new, bubbling wine burst from the fountain's
    summits
Cascading down to the basins. The air was full of grapes
And little birds from afar clustered about their rims,
Not daring to drink, finally, and all was light and wine.
I forgot what we'd felt or said. My trickle of blood had died,
As the light outside seemed to brighten.
                                    Then rest; then five dollars. Then
    Allen
Urged us out onto the street. The wind sang around the
    corner,
Blowing in from the Sound and a siren screeched away

Up Amsterdam Avenue. *Now you have a chocolate malted*
And then you're fine, he said, and the wind blew his hair like
    feathers,
And we both dissolved into nineteen forty-eight, to be whirled
Away into the wildwood of time, I to leave the city
For the disorganized plain, spectre of the long drink
Taken of me that afternoon. *Turning a guy*
On, said Allen last year to the hip psychiatrists
Down in Atlantic City, *that's the most intimate thing*
You can ever do to him. Perhaps. I have bled since
To many cadences, if not to the constant tune
Of the heart's yielding and now I know how hard it is
To turn the drops that leaky faucets make in unquiet
Nights, the discrete tugs of love in its final scene,
Into a stream, whether thicker or thinner than blood, and I
    know
That opening up at all is harder than meeting a measure:
With night coming on like a death, a ruby of blood is a
    treasure.

WEST END BLUES

The neon glow escapes from
Inside; on a cracked red leather
Booth poets are bursting
Into laughter, half in
Death with easeful love. They
Feign mournful ballads
Made to their mistresses' highbrows

"Lalage, I have lain with thee these many nights"
For example (but I hadn't,
Really, only once, and
When we got to the room

I'd borrowed from a logician
We left all the lights off,
And so in the cloudy morning
She gasped at the sudden, grey sight
Of the newspaper picture of Henry
Wallace tacked up on the wall)

You bastards, my girl's in there,
Queening it up in the half-light

O salacious tavern!
Festus taught me the chords of "Milenberg Joys" there
Far from mid-western places where red sunsets fall
Across railroad tracks, beyond the abandoning
Whistles of trains.

They've taken out the bar that lay along the wall
And put one in the middle
Like a bar in Indiana
(Not the old Regulator where there were hardboiled eggs)

"Approchez-vous, Néron, et prenez votre place"
Said Gellius, and there I was, skulking like Barrault
After his big dance in *Les Enfants du Paradis*
When Lemaître takes him out for coffee: "Yes, Ma," I said
While the frightfully rare breed of terrier waddled
From lap to lap, ignoring his dish of sorrowful beer.
And later on in the evening, swimming through the smoke,
Visions of others came upon us as we sat there,
Wondering who we were: Drusus, who followed a dark
Form down along the steps to the water of the river,
Always seemed to have just left for his terrible moment;
Gaius in Galveston, setting out for Dakar,
Was never away. As a bouncy avatar
Of "Bye, Bye Blackbird" flew out of its flaming cage
Of juke-box colored lights yet once more, finally

I would arise in my black raincoat and lurch my way
Out to the street with a shudder. The cold and steamy air
Carrying protein smells from somewhere across the river
Hovered about me, bearing me out of Tonight into
A late hour like any other: as when at five in the morning,
Clatter of milk cans below his window on the street
Measured with hushed, unstressed sounds of her long hair,
Her pillowslip, beside his window on the bed,
Suddenly the exhausted undergraduate sees his prize
Poem taking its shape in a horribly classical meter
—So would the dark of common night well up around me
As the revolving door emptied me onto the street.

Salax taberna! And all you, in there, past the third
Corner away from Athena's corny little owl
Hiding for shame in the academic skirt-folds of Columbia,
Alma Mater, who gazes longingly downtown—
All you, all you in there, lined up along the bar
Or queening it up in the half-light,
Listen to me! No, don't!

Across Broadway and down a bit, the painfully bright
Fluorescence and fierce tile of Bickford's always shone
Omnisciently, and someone sad and crazy said
"God lives in Bickford's"

But that was after we had all become spectres, too,
And eyes, younger eyes, would glisten all unrecognizing
As heads turned,
Interrupting the stories innocently and inaccurately
Being told about us, to watch the revolving door make a tired,
Complete turn, as the shape huddled inside it hardly
Bothered to decide not to go in at all,
Having been steered there only by the heart's mistakes
In the treasonable night; by a kind of broken habit.

GLASS LANDSCAPE

The dreadful fields, all bare of images, are swallowing
Each other up as he vainly tries to outrace them; shallow
Ice-ponds glare; of images there are none, for the eye
To see or the ear to convert. Only the barely-whitening
Sky to the east menaces the plains with the possibility,
Even, of change. His eye, widening at the window, filling
The known world, he decidedly desires to be a dweller
There, outside the mind's landscapes, outside the clear shell
Of the eye. *Ai, ai, I, I,* dust in his ego, unwatered
With spring tears, tears at the vision before him, shattering
The patient perspective, the patent nonsense of there being
Such a thing as transparency. Nothing really important
Lies in the scene beyond the travelling glass before him.
He has something in his eye, something unendurable
By way of a speck. The terrible night of burning eyeball
And flushed lid is upon him, the other eye now filled
With sympathetic brine, and the sea-green plush seat, spilling
Over the interior seen before him, even barer
Of the possibility of any images than his bleared
Eye is barred to delights. Appearances have dimmed
Into unimportance, and pain has pared down all the distance
Into a present point. "Importance isn't important,
"What's important is the truth," said the rather important
Philosopher who suffered, for all his pains. Then the tunnel
Under the long, long hill comes, and outside the running
Glass of the dirty train window, the darkness plummets
Across its blank, unblamed gray eye, neither praising nor
   punishing.

FROM THE RAMBLE

Gracefully touching hands, the three lost, tiny pools
Laughed across open lips of rock between their basins,
Fringed by the dancing late spring grass that barely moved
To the wind's secret music, to the soft, semi-brave
Flashing of sparrows from the glistening mica phrases
Of the gray margins. Gracing all this, the laughter, the sound of
Laughter from where the waters poured from each pool's face
Away toward its sisters, coursed always gently downward,
     Then finally vanishing underground.

From that high, quiet summit, somewhere above the tired,
Parched slope of Burns' Lawn, no voices and no dancing
Of water came; not even in winter, when the thin, bright
Ice snapped like shining foil underfoot, and a trickle chattered,
Almost as if remembered only from louder splashings;
Almost as if in dream, when the wind's secret silence
Flares up as it did in Avignon when the huge swans, sadly
Imponded in the high park, were frozen somehow, wildly,
     Last winter, in the unheard-of ice.

Even in winter, when that slope was always called
Eagle Hill, for the flexible flights of shining children
Shouting down towards the drive, when bare bushes enforced
No secrecy at the top of the hill, the pools still hid.
Unbidden, once, I crept with my sled through drifts and
    thickets
And saw the three asleep, still holding hands beneath
The bluish ice. Imprisoned? No more than my eyes, which,
    stinging
With wind and tears of glare, I lidded down, relieved
     For a dark minute of what I'd seen.

High, high above so many rocks they seemed to lie:
Deep back into the park, beyond the places of

So much adventuring: on chasms of schist, split by
Sheer blows of archaic force, we clambered toward the sun
And dared and chose or sulked alone and sometimes wondered.
Back toward the Ramble, there, as in a hidden garden,
The three of them, ringing the sunlight reflected in their flood
In full spring, dancing, remain beyond the reaches of darkness.
      The ponds, the three, have they departed?

I sought them once in the summer; remembering treacheries
Of remembrance, how what never occurred can usurp the true
Event's privileges, warned that they might not be there,
I climbed upward, in June's more distant margin, through
Tangles of greeny brush toward the places they used
To lie among—past where the twisting path that each winter
Revealed as Snake Hill, white, dangerous and cruel,
Clung to the curving rise, tender, asphalted, innocent,
      Black, in the green of summer's wisdom.

And there they were, still braiding together the rippling water,
Leaping into view as I parted a budding hedge
Like some famous painting one finally sees, abroad,
At the end of a great corridor, bound with a connection
Stronger than merely the old rope of total resemblance
To the reproductions of it one had always known.
As, leaping into view, three graces, dancing, bending
Naked arms in a circle of girl, redeem the mere hopes
      That art books' intimations spoke.

And there they were: the unroaring water flashed, silvery,
And high, hot light shot up from the three shallow bowls,
Surfaces gently amove, one to another spilled:
One giving, one accepting, one returning that flow,
The benefits of the surface, light and awareness thrown
Off them, through the eye, to the overseeing mind—
And all this happening with barely a trace of motion
Across their faces, as if the world had too much light
      Ever to mirror in water shining.

As if the three must be forever almost still,
Fixed like an image so well known that memory
Need never reanimate it even for an instant,
There they were, unchanged, confirmed in their present selves.
Or again: once in another summer, crossing westward,
I entered the Park by an unfamiliar gate, and mounted
A fair rise, crashed through brush, took a wrong path, and
    ended
Up on that eminence of old at a late, late hour,
      Surprised by a distant sound of shouting—

A child's, on Eagle Hill, below my vision—and there
They were, barely enclosed in their modest, open room,
Gaily shaded by hedges interlaced carelessly
With the lowering sunlight. Taken, those unastonished pools,
By surprise, by the wrong approach, they lay as if unperused,
More like themselves than ever, all immediate surface
And rippled whorls of reflection shimmering as if newly
Glimpsed, free of deceit, free of perspective's absurd
      Draperies; smiling; and yet concerned.

And all was silence, save for the roaring of the world
In its turning. As once, not long before, the same smiling
Silence hung in the air around my head, unheard,
While far away beyond the bath-houses the wild
Surf slapped out its breath against the beach with sighs
And long, gasping diastoles; for there, before
My wearied eye at the knot-hole, ringed with noon's high
    sunlight,
The three undressing girls stopped for a moment, awed
      By the quiet air and the sun and all.

And there there there they were, grouped in the narrow locker
Within my breathless ring of vision, unbroken circle
Of heads averted, stretched arms, and all motions stopped,
One from the rear, the others facing me and turned

Gently inward, the gleam of skin and shadow of fur
Giving of all their surfaces, phenomena generous
Beyond deserving, as if the good one did were served
With double return, as if one could face the benefit,
     The moments of light now, the given present.

But all in an instant becomes the past, the intermittent . . .
The given is withdrawn. Whether a meteor trail
A following streak of fire or of searing after-image,
Our very glimpse of it consumes what should remain;
Cumulonimbus gatherings aloft in the blue fail,
Falling in the wind, into senseless blobs of cotton;
Tears dissolve a moment into what hearts can make
Merely memorable, perhaps precious, or even solemn—
     A source turned off, a cycle stopped.

And, as the sad rain, falling at four o'clock in the morning
Renews the half-lit hollow streets, and curling smoke,
Emerging from deep beneath shining surfaces, calls
Only losses to mind, only the last sigh-blown
Touch betwixt cloth and skin, only the last condoling
*"See? We've really lost nothing tonight, because life
Is much too complicated,"* only the leaving, and only
Then the continuing rain outside, barely brightening
     Streets, just darkening hearts, finally—

So with the clear-eyed world, freshly washed of vision.
Three naked girls in the shadows of noon, three shallow basins
Open to all the weathers, fall away into flickering
Points of memory, their substance consumed, their surface
   aflame.
They burn, they burn! So in winter once, I began to trace
Them out again by another unfamiliar route;
Thinking again to regain the withdrawn, the radiant spaces,
The flowered moments and points of joy, I sought my pools,
     Cold at my shoulders, the wind, pursuing.

Cold at my feet, the hard, dry ground at the fringes of the
   Ramble.
Here all the surrounding city is hidden; even in winter
When gray mists seem to condense in bare, unfocused branches,
None of the heights of buildings ringing the park is visible.
There among intricate paths, crossing themselves and twisting
Mazy configurations out of the asphalt walks,
Was the heart of the Park, with its dells and bridges over the
   inlet;
There was the final garden, full of the planned disorder,
     Of the garden regained, forced and sprawling.

Cold at my heart, the climbing slowly west and upward,
Away from one Museum with a painted past behind me
Toward the other's boundless pictures—cases of animals stuffed
From which I learned to read all landscapes and to climb
Inside all painted prospects, into their hidden lives.
Cold at my ears, I moved toward the huge, dark halls
Of skull-formed Africa where I had roamed, in childhood,
A wondering traveller along those mental shores;
     Cold at my eyes, I walked and walked.

And there they were, but not as they had been remembered,
Two hardly distinguishable, the third dried-out and muddy,
Misshapen clumps of puddle, they lay, a visionary
Disaster, before me, my eyes bleared and my heart fluttering—
As if the recollected surfaces had sunk
Down into crusty sockets of earth, ringed with sparse and
Dried-out grass, the given presence absorbed by dull,
Treasureless mines that the thirsty, chilling present park's
     Ground all had come to, dark and hard.

Mud at my heart, I could only stare, then turn to the east and
Vanish into the Ramble, losing the misplaced
And badly recollected pools behind me, even
As the city itself was hidden behind the narrow frame

And binding horizons of trees and underbrush. I made
My way across the cold, unfeeling paths that twist
About through the real distances, and finally came
Out of the park, into the unmistakeable city
     Safe for the heart, because unenvisioned.

—Not like some misremembered loveliness of trees
Bare, for instance, of leaf in misty February:
Their blackish filaments, plane behind plane, receding
Into the general and dissolving gray, are melted
Down to remembrances of branches, to negatives,
To losses. I coughed in the fumes of traffic, as around me
Windows and parking-lights and other presences
Emitted a world I was hardly grateful for. It crowded
     Behind my eyes in that darkening hour.

As if the pools had vanished into the unabsorbent
Ground, I would avoid for months and months thereafter
The eminence they'd lain upon, now always courting
Other corners of path and bench and brush, the Ramble
Springing to green and filling the sky's borders with splashes
Of decoration. Down in some dirty dale, all hunched
Into a fading bench, time after time I sat
Brooding over the few pictures of those sunken
     Pools I had kept untorn and uncluttered.

And once I walked toward where I pictured them separated
By clumps of protecting privet, emerging, as once ascended,
In tiers, first one, then, hidden, the second giving way
Immediately to one more, facing off to the west.
Having gained the last height there, I turned toward the setting
Sun, behind the pairs of towers that guard the rim
Of the visible—the modernistic CENTURY, the stubby
  MAJESTIC
And gold-painted SAN REMO, and uptown at the edge of
  vision,
     EL DORADO'S pinnacles springing

Skyward,—then penetrate the great blue open room
Where all the sunsets burn; downward they disappear
In unseen chambers of bedrock; outward, already ruins
Of a wild, recent time, evoking all their fearful
Doubles in Moscow; branchless stumps ringing a clearing
In irony's forest. But inward, they glow in the dying sun
To cauterize the winds that make them matter and give
Them meaning: all the sad, ugly towers, mortared with mud,
    Moribund, crumbling into dust.

Even at dawn, even at fairer moments than these
Glimpses out at the boundaries of all this ruined garden
Reveal a city to be achieved, the towers unreal,
The glittering windows unapproachable, the far
Finials and fretwork lifted almost to the stars
Beyond even their own vulgarity, beyond
The gestures of aspiration that left them scattered, sparkling
At all the irrational hours, hung high, but yet unpromised
    There where only the eye can follow.

Once even at the false sunset inside the plated dome
Of the planetarium, when night falls far too soon,
The bungled silhouetted mockups of all those
Surrounding towers, unbelievable and crude,
Taught me to watch the slower vanishings at the true
Rim of the park at dusk. At dusk in our present time,
Too, we learn of our sick condition: the senseless, the cruel,
The angry and the deprived roam through the lack of light,
    Smashing the benefits long denied them.

So frowning violence reassumes the crowded land,
And silently, as afternoon unfolds its shades,
Boys with corrupted terriers wander among the Ramble's
Winding and convoluted walks. In the terminating
Spring's convulsive heat, shouts drift up, then fade
Over the nearby water, and even to have remembered

Light leaping up like laughter from three surfaces, breaking
Out of those lost ponds into the shining air, is a blessing.
  Have I a right to demand their presence?

I must deserve such benefits, such pools of water, such frail
Surfaces of delight, whether remembered by
Mistake, or really received, deserved not by laboring
Merely, but by a readiness of the heart to accept such fine
Gifts of phenomena. To what have I been entitled?
A loan of three ponds, perhaps. A gift of light over snow
In the glare of December sun. A solemn launch, gliding
Among rowboats. Discoveries of love on dark October
  Benches beneath smashed lamppost globes.

—To a glimpse more precious, even, than those of goldenmost
 towers.
When, once at hide-and-seek, by a path, that ran below
The crown of hill engemmed with ponds that I'd not found
Out for myself yet, I pushed through a hedge of broken
Privet and fell headlong against the concrete and oaken
Bench, where a tall fat man I now guess was thirty-five
Or thereabouts, was stretched, brooding, with his whole
Length extended along the bench, his head supported
  Not with his palm, along the jaw,

But on his wrist and the back of his hand, his fingertips
Continuing past his chin; and he lay on his left side
And watched me as I rubbed my scraped brow with my mitten.
And from where I stood, I read on his face the kind of smile,
Awkward, a little strained, that one can often find
In mirrors; and as the wind blew dead leaves on the path
Tangling his long, untidy hair, I turned, and behind me
He lay there motionless. I felt him bless me. I ran
  Away from the vision behind my back.

What did he see, that lying man? A boy, running
Down along an airless path between scrubby trees?
Three silent children playing in a ring, then? Something
Utterly different, rising behind his eyesight weeks
Later and then forever? For whatever he had received,
Oh let him have been thankful, even as I am now:
It is a garden we fall from; a city, somehow, we feel
That we have been promised, though not a city built to
   surround
        A park, a remembered past like ours;

It is a garden inside a city I will have remembered,
And three small pools I will remember having imagined
As gracing the top of an undistinguished eminence
Not too high in that park. Lying now in the grass,
Cool in the light of July on a sward long past
Burns' Lawn, we fasten our tired gaze, she and I,
Across the trees to the west, framing our world in a vast
Moment of stillness. This night, this newly darkened sky,
        This scarred park rolling out behind us,

Even this city itself, are ours, wholly unshared
Because unremembered except by both of us, who have made
Light come into darkness, graces dance on a bare
Hilltop, a cycle of months spin around on a frail
Wheel of language and touch. O see this light! As a blaze
Of cloud above the western towers gleams for an instant
Up there! Firing the sky, higher than it should be able
To reach, a single firework launched from the unseen river
        Rises and dies, as we kiss and listen.

From Movie-Going and Other Poems

MOVIE-GOING

Drive-ins are out, to start with. One must always be
Able to see the over-painted Moorish ceiling
Whose pinchbeck jazz gleams even in the darkness, calling
The straying eye to feast on it, and glut, then fall
Back to the sterling screen again. One needs to feel
That the two empty, huddled, dark stage-boxes keep
Empty for kings. And having frequently to cope
With the abominable goodies, overflow
Bulk and (finally) exploring hands of flushed
Close neighbors gazing beadily out across glum
Distances is, after all, to keep the gleam
Alive of something rather serious, to keep
Faith, perhaps, with the City. When as children our cup
Of joys ran over the special section, and we clutched
Our ticket stubs and followed the bouncing ball, no clash
Of cymbals at the start of the stage-show could abash
Our third untiring time around. When we came back,
Older, to cop an endless series of feels, we sat
Unashamed beneath the bare art-nouveau bodies, set
High on the golden, after-glowing proscenium when
The break had come. And still, now as always, once
The show is over and we creep into the dull
Blaze of mid-afternoon sunshine, the hollow dole
Of the real descends on everything and we can know
That we have been in some place wholly elsewhere, a night
At noonday, not without dreams, whose portals shine
(Not ivory, not horn in ever-changing shapes)
But made of some weird, clear substance not often used for
    gates.
Stay for the second feature on a double bill
Always: it will teach you how to love, how not to live,
And how to leave the theater for that unlit, aloof
And empty world again. "B"-pictures showed us: shooting

More real than singing or making love; the shifting
Ashtray upon the mantel, moved by some idiot
Between takes, helping us learn beyond a trace of doubt
How fragile are imagined scenes; the dimming-out
Of all the brightness of the clear and highly lit
Interior of the hero's cockpit, when the stock shot
Of ancient dive-bombers peeling off cuts in, reshapes
Our sense of what is, finally, plausible; the grays
Of living rooms, the blacks of cars whose window glass
At night allows the strips of fake Times Square to pass
Jerkily by on the last ride; even the patch
Of sudden white, and inverted letters dashing
Up during the projectionist's daydream, dying
Quickly—these are the colors of our inner life.

Never ignore the stars, of course. But above all,
Follow the asteroids as well: though dark, they're more
Intense for never glittering; anyone can admire
Sparklings against a night sky, but against a bright
Background of prominence, to feel the Presences burnt
Into no fiery fame should be a more common virtue.
For, just as Vesta has no atmosphere, no verdure
Burgeons on barren Ceres, bit-players never surge
Into the rhythms of expansion and collapse, such
As all the flaming bodies live and move among.
But there, more steadfast than stars are, loved for their being,
Not for their burning, move the great Characters: see
Thin Donald Meek, that shuffling essence ever so
Affronting to Eros and to Pride; the pair of bloated
Capitalists, Walter Connolly and Eugene Pallette, seated
High in their offices above New York; the evil,
Blackening eyes of Sheldon Leonard, and the awful
Stare of Eduardo Cianelli. Remember those who have gone—
(Where's bat-squeaking Butterfly McQueen? Will we see again
That ever-anonymous drunk, waxed-moustached, rubber-legged
Caught in revolving doors?) and think of the light-years logged

Up in those humbly noble orbits, where no hot
Spotlight of solar grace consumes some blazing hearts,
Bestowing the flimsy immortality of stars
For some great distant instant. Out of the darkness stares
Venus, who seems to be what once we were, the fair
Form of emerging love, her nitrous atmosphere
Hiding her prizes. Into the black expanse peers
Mars, whom we in time will come to resemble: parched,
Xanthine desolations, dead Cimmerian seas, the far
Distant past preserved in the blood-colored crusts; fire
And water both remembered only. Having shined
Means having died. But having been real only, and shunned
Stardom, the planetoids are what we now are, humming
With us, above us, ever into the future, seeming
Ever to take the shapes of the world we wake to from dreams.

Always go in the morning if you can; it will
Be something more than habit if you do. Keep well
Away from most French farces. Try to see a set
Of old blue movies every so often, that the sight
Of animal doings out of the clothes of 'thirty-five
May remind you that even the natural act is phrased
In the terms and shapes of particular times and places.
Finally, remember always to honor the martyred dead.
The forces of darkness spread everywhere now, and the best
And brightest screens fade out, while many-antennaed beasts
Perch on the housetops, and along the grandest streets
Palaces crumble, one by one. The dimming starts
Slowly at first; the signs are few, as "Movies are
Better than Ever," "Get More out of Life. See a Movie" Or
Else there's no warning at all and, Whoosh! the theater falls,
Alas, transmogrified: no double-feature fills
A gleaming marquee with promises, now only lit
With "Pike and Whitefish Fresh Today" "Drano" and "Light
Or Dark Brown Sugar, Special." Try never to patronize
Such places (or pass them by one day a year). The noise

Of movie mansions changing form, caught in the toils
Of our lives' withering, rumbles, resounds and tolls
The knell of neighborhoods. Do not forget the old
Places, for everyone's home has been a battlefield.

I remember: the RKO COLONIAL; the cheap
ARDEN and ALDEN both; LOEW's LINCOLN SQUARE's bright shape;
The NEWSREEL; the mandarin BEACON, resplendently arrayed;
The tiny SEVENTY-SEVENTH STREET, whose demise I rued
So long ago; the eighty-first street, sunrise-hued,
RKO; and then LOEW's at eighty-third, which had
The colder pinks of sunset on it; and then, back
Across Broadway again, and up, you disembarked
At the YORKTOWN and then the STODDARD, with their dark
Marquees; the SYMPHONY had a decorative disk
With elongated 'twenties nudes whirling in it;
(Around the corner the THALIA, daughter of memory! owed
Her life to Foreign Hits, in days when you piled your coat
High on your lap and sat, sweating and cramped, to catch
"La Kermesse Heroique" every third week, and watched
Fritz Lang from among an audience of refugees, bewitched
By the sense of Crisis on and off that tiny bit
Of screen) Then north again: the RIVERSIDE, the bright
RIVIERA rubbing elbows with it; and right
Smack on a hundredth street, the MIDTOWN; and the rest
Of them: the CARLTON, EDISON, LOEW's OLYMPIA, and best
Because, of course, the last of all, its final burst
Anonymous, the NEMO! These were once the pearls
Of two-and-a-half miles of Broadway! How many have paled
Into a supermarket's failure of the imagination?

Honor them all. Remember how once their splendor blazed
In sparkling necklaces across America's blasted
Distances and deserts: think how, at night, the fastest
Train might stop for water somewhere, waiting, faced
Westward, in deepening dusk, till ruby illuminations

Of something different from Everything Here, Now, shine
Out from the local Bijou, truest gem, the most bright
Because the most believed in, staving off the night
Perhaps, for a while longer with its flickering light.

These fade. All fade, Let us honor them with our own fading
   sight.

ARISTOTLE TO PHYLLIS

for Rogers Albritton

(*The 14th century legend of Aristotle and the girl sometimes called Campaspe exemplified the frailty of pagan
learning and the power of Amor. Represented in medieval
sculpture by a beaming court-lady astride a solemn scholar,
the story is later illustrated by a modish whore forcing a
nasty old man to carry her piggy-back in the work of
Northern engravers like Urs Graf, Baldung Grien and
Lucas Van Leyden around the turn of the sixteenth century. The speaker in this poem is a composite of the medieval cleric and the lascivious humanist of the later pictures.
Meden agan: the famous "nothing in excess" of the
Greeks.)*

This chair I trusted, lass, and I looted the leaves
   Of my own sense and of clerks' learning, lessened
The distance towards the end of my allotted eyesight
   Over dull treatises on Reason and
Sensuality, learning very little about
   What can still happen on a summer morning.
Faint sea-breezes, when felt too far inland, sometimes
   Smack bone-deep, bruise marine depths, somersault
Into a flood of sick sea-longing. You walked past
   The window where my writing desk stands thick
And oaken, jammed against the mullioned lights, and where
   A pitch pine litters all my work with fragrance
Once too often. If all beauty is scale and order,
   Well then, the old man is unbeautiful
In outraging his age, that should be past all dancing,
   Playing all too well the infidel sage
Unwilling even to gamble on a Final Life
   That is no sleep. And this being so, a simple
Country matter can be so urgent, and a piece
   Of tumble, bubbly breasts and trollopy

Lurch, can matter so much. So little can be said
 For you, except that you're alive. But such
A question, with the right wind freshening from the sea
 Blows back and forth across the mind: the bright
Emphatic mosses, furring the cracks along the garden
 Wall, trembling in the touch of breeze and blurring
The surface of the masonry, fill all the sight.
 But still, trained in restraint and reared in reason,
I sit at my desk, half in death, and staring down at
 A wide papyrus, silenced, blanched and deafened
To pleas for eloquence, its face pale with long darkness:
 Some other age must smash its last defense.
We're no historians; what's past has faded, died, and
 Lingers no more; and only its remains
Appear in patchworks of quotation, as in all
 The fussy, fretted centos that I have
Assembled from the poets. Even here (and you
 Must get the scribe who reads you this to show
Them all to you) the tessellated lines of one
 Whose greatest voyages involved the vessel
From which he dipped pale ink of an exotic nature,
 Appear; but in my language all these sink
Into an earthier journey. A few swift rounds
 Under the evergreens outside; the fir
And box-hedge hiding us, clouds peering in the pool
 To view gardens reflected, and the yews
Along the wall waving green, encouraging brushes;
 Come, Phyllis, come; the miles I have been saving
Are for your travelling. Only in middle age
 Did *meden agan* amount to anything.
Come away! pass the mead again; and gathering
 Your thick skirts bellyward, lean back and lead
Me, simpering, outside into the garden. There
 As you throw up your leg to climb astride
My back, I'll dutifully munch the bit; then bottom
 To bottom, will the no-backed beast run, duly

Peripatetic at each mossy garden corner.
    Giddyap, good Doctor! If by chance the static
And pungent waters of the garden pool reveal
    Our natures to our eyes, it's all part of
The party, eh? Stammering, balanced, the master
    Of those who know, old staggerer, not bearing
A chubby giggling slut merely, but rather, like
    Some fabled, prudent beast that bears with it
Its water, nutriment or home, will carry then
    The bed he'll soon board. Underneath a tent
Of cherried branches ripening fast, I'll put you to
    The plow, and turn your furrows up, and Spring,
Spring will envelop all the air. From far across
    The wall a scent of distant pines will fall
Even as now it drops across my writing desk,
    Full of reports of distant life, and hopes
Regained, and projects floated on an unnavigable
    Future. And whether there will be a fated
Sea fight tomorrow, exploding, showering results
    On the ignoring water, or merely a plodding
And serious fool about to quarrel with a colleague
    Over what once I might have meant (devout
Enough, both of them, although never having learned
    The tongue I write in) cannot be told now.
But at the brink of the moment, mad, mad, for its coming,
    Our knowledge quickens, ripping at the garment
That cloaks the truth that will be. Let's get on with it,
    The game in which the master turns the silly
Ass, straining for breath, arousing the outraged gales of
    What should have been a season of calm weather.

HOBBES, 1651

When I returned at last from Paris hoofbeats pounded
    Over the harsh and unrelenting road;
It was cold, the snow high; I was old, and the winter
    Sharp, and the dead mid-century sped by
In ominous, blurred streaks as, brutish, the wind moaned
    Among black branches. I rode through a kind
Of graceless winter nature, bled of what looked like life.
    My vexing horse threw me. If it was not safe
In England yet, or ever, that nowhere beneath the gray
    Sky would be much safer seemed very plain.

DIGGING IT OUT

The icicle finger of death, aimed
At the heart always, melts in the sun
But here at night, now with the porchlight
Spilling over the steps, making snow
More marmoreal than the moon could,
It grows longer and, as it lengthens,
Sharpens. All along the street cars are
Swallowed up in the sarcophagous
Mounds, and digging out had better start
Now, before the impulse to work dies,
Frozen into neither terror nor
Indifference, but a cold longing
For sleep. After a few shovelfuls,
Chopped, pushed, then stuck in a hard white fudge,
Temples pound; the wind scrapes icily
Against the beard of sweat already
Forming underneath most of my face,

And halting for a moment's only
Faltering, never resting. There is
Only freezing here, no real melting
While the thickening silence slows up
The motion of the very smallest
Bits of feeling, even.
                              Getting back
To digging's easier than stopping.
Getting back to the unnerving snow
Seems safer than waiting while the rush
Of blood inside one somewhere, crazed by
The shapes one has allowed his life to
Take, throbs, throbs and threatens. If my heart
Attack itself here in the whitened
Street, would there be bugles and the sound
Of hoofbeats thumping on a hard-packed,
Shiny road of snow? Or is that great
Onset of silences itself a
Great white silence? The crunching of wet
Snow around my knees seems louder, now
That the noises of the fear and what the
Fear is of are louder too, and in
The presence of such sounding depths of
Terror, it is harder than ever
To believe what I have always heard:
That it feels at first like spasms of
Indigestion. The thought, as one shoves
Scrapingly at the snow that always
Seems to happen to things and places
That have been arranged just so, the thought
Of being able to wonder if
Something I'd eaten had disagreed
With me, the while waiting to die, is
Ridiculous. "Was it something I
Felt?" "Something I knew?" "Something I was?"
Seem more the kind of thing that one might

Wonder about, smiling mildly, as
He fell gently no great distance to
The cushioning world that he had dug.
Silently—for to call out something
In this snow would be to bury it.
And heavily, for the weight of self
Is more, perhaps at the end, than can
Be borne.
       No, it is only now, as
I urge the bending blade beneath a
Snow-packed tire for what I know can
Not be the last time that I whimper:
I hate having to own a car; I
Don't want to dig it out of senseless
Snow; I don't want to have to die, snow
Or no snow. As the wind blows up a
Little, fine, white powders are sprinkled
Across the clear windshield. Down along
The street a rustle of no leaves comes
From somewhere. And as I realize
What rest is, pause, and start in on a
New corner, I seem to know that there
Is no such thing as overtaxing,
That digging snow is a rhythm, like
Breathing, loving and waiting for night
To end or, much the same, to begin.

A LION NAMED PASSION

". . . the girl had walked past several cages occupied by other lions before she was seized by a lion named Passion. It was from his cage that keepers recovered the body."
THE NEW YORK TIMES, *May 16, 1958*

Hungering on the gray plain of its birth
For the completion of the sunny cages
To hold all its unruly, stretching forth
Its longest streets and narrowest passages,
The growing city paws the yielding earth,
And rears its controlling stones. Its snarl damages
The dull, unruffled fabric of silences
In which the world is wrapped. The day advances
And shadows lengthen as their substances
Grow more erect and rigid, as low hearth
And high, stark tower rise beneath the glances
Of anxious, ordered Supervision. North
Bastion and eastern wall are joined, and fences
Are finished between the areas of Mirth
And the long swards of Mourning. Growth manages
At once vigor of spurts, and rigor of stages.

If not the Just City, then the Safe one: sea
And mountain torrent warded off, and all
The wildest monsters caged, that running free,
The most exposed and open children shall
Fear no consuming grasp. Thus the polity
Preserves its fast peace by the burial
Of these hot barbarous sparks whose fiery, bright
Eruption might disturb blackness of night
And temperateness of civil love. The light
Of day is light enough, calm, gray, cozy
And agreeable. And beasts? The lion might

Be said to dwell here, but so tamed is he,
—Set working in the streets, say, with no fright
Incurred by these huge paws which turn with glee
A hydrant valve, while playing children sprawl
And splash to the bright spray, dribbling a shiny ball—

So innocent he is, his huge head, high
And chinny, pointed over his shoulder, more
A lion rampant, blazoned on the sky,
Than monster romping through the streets, with gore
Reddening his jaws; so kind of eye
And clear of gaze is that sweet beast, that door
Need never shut, nor window bar on him.
But look! Look there! One morning damp and dim
In thick, gray fog, or even while the slim
And gaily tigering shadows creep on by
The porch furniture on hot noons, see him
Advancing through the streets, with monstrous cry,
Half plea, half threat, dying in huff of flame!
This must be some new beast! As parents spy,
Safe, from behind parked cars, he damps his roar—
It is the little children he is making for!

When elders, not looking at each other, creep
Out of their hiding places, little men,
Little women, stare back, resentment deep
Inside their throats at what had always been
A Great Place for the Kids: infants asleep
And growing, boys and girls, all, all eaten,
Burned by the prickly heat of baby throbbing,
Already urging scratching hands; the sobbing
After certain hot hurts in childhood; stabbing
Pulses and flashing floods of summer that leap
Out, in the dusk of childhood, at youth, dabbing
At the old wounds from which fresh feelings seep.
"O help me! I am being done!" the bobbing

Hip and awakened leg, one day, from heap
Of melting body call. Done? No, undone!
Robbing the grave of first fruits, the beast feeds again.

Burning is being consumed by flaming beasts,
Rebellious and unappeasable. The wind
Of very early morning, finally, casts
A cool sweet quenching draught on hunger's end,
Those ashes and whitened bones. Each day, to lists
Of dead and sorely wounded are assigned
The tasks of memory. Mute crowds push by
The useless cages and restraining, high,
(But not retaining) walls. Against the sky
Only these ruins show at dawn, like masts,
Useless in ships becalmed, but hung with dry
Corpses, or like unheeded fruit that blasts
High in trees, wasted. Menacing, wild of eye,
The city, having missed its spring, now feasts,
Nastily, on itself. Jackals attend
The offal. And new cities raven and distend.

OFF MARBLEHEAD

A woeful silence, following in our wash,
fills the thick, fearful roominess, blanketing
    bird noise and ocean splash; thus, always
        soundlessly, rounding the point we go

gliding by dippy, quizzical cormorants.
One black maneuver moving them all at once,
    they turn their beaks to windward then, and,
        snubbing the gulls on the rocks behind them,

point, black, a gang of needles against the gray
dial sky, as if some knowledge, some certainty
    could now be read therefrom. And if we
        feel that the meter may melt, those thin necks

droop, numbers vanish from the horizon when
we turn our heads to scribble the reading down
    on salty, curled, dried pages, it is
        merely our wearied belief, our strained and

ruining grasp of what we assume, that blurs
our eyes and blears the scene that surrounds us: tears
    of spray, the long luff's reflex flapping,
        crazy with pain, and the clenching sheet,

and, looming up, Great Misery (Named for whose?
When?) Island. Groaning, jangling in irons, crews
    of gulls still man a rolling buoy not
        marked on our charts. Overhead, the light

(impartial, general, urging of no new course)
spares no approving brightening for the sparse
    and sorry gains of one we hold to
        now, ever doubting our memory. But

no matter—whether running before the wind
away for home, or beating against the end
    of patience, toward its coastline, still the
        movement is foolishly close to one of

flight, the thick, oily clouds undissolving, crowds
of sea birds, senseless, shrill, unappeased, no boats
    about, and, out to sea, a sickening,
        desperate stretch of unending dark.

RACE ROCK LIGHT

Over sparkling and green water, the lighthouse seems
Smaller than what the sun, pouring about our cupped,
    Shading hands, should contract it
        To; and glaring reflections, splashed

Off the top of the bright bay just at noon are like
Guarding pulses that cut visions to size, adjust
    Shapes of images, lest they
        Seem to matter too much in fresh

Sunlight shining across prospects of summer shores'
Middle distances. Set out on a lump of wet
    Rock, a commonly ugly
        House, mansarded and squat, affronts

Any view of the bay; crowded inside a space
Far too small to surround it, the unlikely house
    Carries, stuck in its roof, a
        Lantern, just as if any fool

Knew "a house plus a light equals a lighthouse." (Eyes,
Minds and voices surmount ignorant bodies, and crowd
    Out on top just as oddly,
        Though) Remembering times one got

Close to there in a boat, straining against the cold
Wind at sundown to see what he could see, one feels
    Puzzled over the keepers
        Living here in a house at sea.

Lighthouse-keeping is like gardening here, inside
Narrow confines of rock, water and sky: the sod
    Growing thick in the perfect
        First of gardens was never churned

Harder than the alarmed Sound in the rake of harsh
Squalls; and Adam could earn Paradise as he served
    No more wisely and well than
        Those who were planted here to tend

Garden, beacon and house. Reddening, now, and proud
Past enduring, that house looks at the sundown hour
    Even more like the scene of
        That original dying dream:

Where those beautiful first children are taking turns
Playing being two bad parents, the sunset fast
    Making green all the shadows,
        Picking out in the window glass

Children's faces, who wait deep in neglect, for rain,
Pouring down on the yard, sending the two ungarbed
    Figures into the house once
        More, where shadows are always brown,

Their light housekeeping doomed always to leave each room,
House or garden or land messier than the last,
    Finally ending with such a
        Place as this one toward evening. Shut

Into houses that keep whatever gardens they need
Locked inside their own walls, herded on rocks that force
    Heavy currents to race on
        By, at least for a while, we make

All our moments of light justify the despised
Houses holding aloft lenses that turn toward shores
    Ranged behind them in darkness,
        Leaving them with a dying mark.

From A Crackling of Thorns

FOR BOTH OF YOU, THE DIVORCE BEING FINAL

We cannot celebrate with doleful Music
The old, gold panoplies that are so great
To sit and watch; but on the other hand,
To command the nasal krummhorns to be silent,
The *tromba marina* to wail; to have the man
Unlatch the tail gate on his cart, permitting
The sackbut player to extend his slide
And go to work on whimpering divisions;
For us to help prepare the masque itself,
Rigging machinery to collapse the household
Just at the end, rehearsing urchins who
Will trip, all gilded, into the master bedroom
And strip the sheets, is, finally, to confess
That what we lack are rituals adequate
To things like this.
                              We tell some anxious friends
"*Basta!* They know what they are doing"; others
Whom we dislike and who, like queens, betray
Never a trace of uneasiness, we play with:
"No, it could never work, my dears, from the start.
We all knew that. Yes, there's the boy to think of,"
And so on. Everyone makes us nervous. Then,
For a dark instant, as in your unlit foyer
At sundown, bringing a parcel, we see you both
And stifle the awkward question: "What, are *you* here?"
Not because it has been asked before
By Others meeting Underground, but simply
Because we cannot now know which of you
Should answer, or even which of you we asked.
We wait for something to happen in the brown
Shadows around us. Surely there is missing
A tinkle of cymbals to strike up the dirge

And some kind of sounding brass to follow it,
Some hideous and embarrassing gimmick which
Would help us all behave less civilly and
More gently, who mistook civility
So long for lack of gentleness.
                                    And since
Weeping's a thing we can no longer manage,
We must needs leave you to the Law's directive:
"You have unmade your bed, now lie about it."
Quickly now: which of you will keep the *Lares,*
Which the *Penates?* And opening the door
We turn like guilty children, mutter something,
And hide in the twilit street.
                                    Along the river
The sky is purpling and signs flash out
And on, to beckon the darkness: THE TIME IS NOW . . .
(What time, what time?) Who stops to look in time
Ever, ever? We can do nothing again
For both of you together. And if I burn
An epithalamium six years old to prove
That what we learn is in some way a function
Of what we forget, I know that I should never
Mention it to anyone. When men
Do in the sunny Plaza what they did
Only in dusky corners before, the sunset
Comes as no benison, the assuring license
Of the June night goes unobserved. The lights
Across the river are brighter than the stars;
The water is black and motionless; whatever
Has happened to all of us, it is too late
For something else ever to happen now.

THE LADY'S-MAID'S SONG

When Adam found his rib was gone
  He cursed and sighed and cried and swore
And looked with cold resentment on
  The creature God had used it for.
All love's delights were quickly spent
  And soon his sorrows multiplied:
He learned to blame his discontent
  On something stolen from his side.

And so in every age we find
  Each Jack, destroying every Joan,
Divides and conquers womankind
  In vengeance for his missing bone.
By day he spins out quaint conceits
  With gossip, flattery, and song,
But then at night, between the sheets,
  He wrongs the girl to right the wrong.

Though shoulder, bosom, lip, and knee
  Are praised in every kind of art,
Here is love's true anatomy:
  His rib is gone; he'll have her heart.
So women bear the debt alone
  And live eternally distressed,
For though we throw the dog his bone
  He wants it back with interest.

For *The Man of Mode*

LATE AUGUST ON THE LIDO

To lie on these beaches for another summer
Would not become them at all,
And yet the water and her sands will suffer
When, in the fall,
These golden children will be taken from her.

It is not the gold they bring: enough of that
Has shone in the water for ages
And in the bright theater of Venice at their backs;
But the final stages
Of all those afternoons when they played and sat

And waited for a beckoning wind to blow them
Back over the water again
Are scenes most necessary to this ocean.
What actors then
Will play when these disperse from the sand below them?

All this is over until, perhaps, next spring;
This last afternoon must be pleasing.
Europe, Europe is over, but they lie here still,
While the wind, increasing,
Sands teeth, sands eyes, sands taste, sands everything.

A THEORY OF WAVES

Having no surface of its own, the pond,
Under the shifting grey contingency
Of morning mists, extends even beyond
The swamp beside it, until presently
The thinning air declares itself to be

No longer water, and the pond itself
Is still for a moment, and no longer air.
Then waking bass glide from their sandy shelf,
And sets of concentric circles everywhere
Expand through some imaginary thing
Whose existence must be assumed, until they meet,
When incorporeal ripples, ring on ring,
Disturb a real surface, as if, with dripping feet,
Some dark hypothesis had made retreat.

THE GREAT BEAR

Even on clear nights, lead the most supple children
Out onto hilltops, and by no means will
They make it out. Neither the gruff round image
From a remembered page nor the uncertain
Finger tracing that image out can manage
To mark the lines of what ought to be there,
Passing through certain bounding stars, until
The whole massive expanse of bear appear
Swinging, across the ecliptic; and, although
The littlest ones say nothing, others respond,
Making us thankful in varying degrees
For what we would have shown them: "There it is!"
"I see it now!" Even "Very like a bear!"
Would make us grateful. Because there is no bear

We blame our memory of the picture: trudging
Up the dark, starlit path, stooping to clutch
An anxious hand, perhaps the outline faded
Then; perhaps could we have retained the thing
In mind ourselves, with it we might have staged
Something convincing. We easily forget
The huge, clear, homely dipper that is such

An event to reckon with, an object set
Across the space the bear should occupy;
But even so, the trouble lies in pointing
At any stars. For one's own finger aims
Always elsewhere: the man beside one seems
Never to get the point. "No! The bright star
Just above my fingertip." The star,

If any, that he sees beyond one's finger
Will never be the intended one. To bring
Another's eye to bear in such a fashion
On any single star seems to require
Something very like a constellation
That both habitually see at night;
Not in the stars themselves, but in among
Their scatter, perhaps, some old familiar sight
Is always there to take a bearing from.
And if the smallest child of all should cry
Out on the wet, black grass because he sees
Nothing but stars, though claiming that there is
Some bear not there that frightens him, we need
Only reflect that we ourselves have need

Of what is fearful (being really nothing)
With which to find our way about the path
That leads back down the hill again, and with
Which to enable the older children standing
By us to follow what we mean by "This
Star," "That one," or "The other one beyond it."
But what of the tiny, scared ones?—Such a bear,
Who needs it? We can still make do with both
The dipper that we always knew was there
And the bright, simple shapes that suddenly
Emerge on certain nights. To understand
The signs that stars compose, we need depend
Only on stars that are entirely there
And the apparent space between them. There

Never need be lines between them, puzzling
Our sense of what is what. What a star does
Is never to surprise us as it covers
The center of its patch of darkness, sparkling
Always, a point in one of many figures.
One solitary star would be quite useless,
A frigid conjecutre, true but trifling;
And any single sign is meaningless
If unnecessary. Crab, bull, and ram,
Or frosty, irregular polygons of our own
Devising, or finally the Great Dark Bear
That we can never quite believe is there—
Having the others, any one of them
Can be dispensed with. The bear, of all of them,

Is somehow most like any one, taken
At random, in that we always tend to say
That just because it might be there; because
Some Ancients really traced it out, a broken
And complicated line, webbing bright stars
And fainter ones together; because a bear
Habitually appeared—then even by day
It is for us a thing that should be there.
We should not want to train ourselves to see it.
The world is everything that happens to
Be true. The stars at night seem to suggest
The shapes of what might be. If it were best,
Even, to have it there (such a great bear!
All hung with stars!), there still would be no bear.

NOTES

KINNERET   The disjunct form of these quatrains is borrowed from the Malay *pantun* (not from its fussy, refrain-plagued nineteenth-century French derivative, the *pantoum*): the first and second lines frame one sentence, and the next two another, apparently unrelated, one. The two are superficially connected by cross-rhyming, and by some common construction, scheme, pun, assonance, or the like and, below the surface, by some puzzlingly deeper parable. Thus a self-descriptive example:

CATAMARAN
Pantuns in the original Malay
Are quatrains of two thoughts, but of one mind.
Athwart these two pontoons I sail away,
Yet touching neither; land lies far behind.

POWERS OF THIRTEEN:

6: "altogether inconvenient ... memory", George Eliot, *Daniel Deronda*.

11: "*M'aidez!*" the cry of distress, became "Mayday," the international signal of same.

12: cf. Emerson, "Hamatreya."

21: The hexagram made of the stars of the thirteen original colonies is on The Great Seal of the United States, verso (see a dollar bill, verso).

22: Zechariah 5:1; Ezekiel 3:1.

27: $28,561 = 13^4$

39: George Santayana would tear signatures out of books for his day's reading in the Pincio in Rome, disposing of them after perusal.

44–45: Philemon and Baucis.

47: He looks like Walt Whitman from a distance.

51: A sonnet is buried here.

52: The Thames in Connecticut is pronounced as written, /θeymz/; the Jordan is a stream running through the campus of Indiana University.

56: The parabola is rather like Saarinen's in St. Louis.

68: The names of many letters of the Hebrew alphabet are dispersed throughout.

73: Viola to Feste: "They that dally nicely with words may quickly make them wanton".

78: The sonnets of Meredith's *Modern Love* have 16 lines.

85: Line 7 is (needless to say?) the middle line of the poem.

101: A wise Duke—such as Federigo da Montefeltro.

109–111: After, long after, the twelfth-century providential hymn, *ki hinne cachomer*.

117: "Either because . . . had" is Hazlitt on *Paradise Regained*.

131: "*Cras amet qui nunquam amavit quiquam amavit cras amet*" is the formerly famous refrain of the *Pervigilium Veneris* ("Those who never loved before will love tomorrow; those used to loving will to-morrow come to love").

133: Acephalic iambic through line 7.

150: The "curious perfume" and the "most melodious twang" are from John Aubrey's digression from his briefest life, of one Nicholas Towes.

163: The acrostic can be seen at once. The terminal letters' acrostic is for Your eyes only.

166: The rhymes on red and white perhaps need not be pointed out; the blue rhymes do indeed mark out the field in the upper left.

BLUE WINE   I visited Saul Steinberg one afternoon and found that he had pasted some mock (or rather, visionary) wine labels on bottles, which were then filled with a substance I could not identify. This poem is an attempt to make sense out of what was apparently in them. In the mock-Homeric part of the poem, *Bhel* is named for the Indo-European base for "bright" or "shining," and *Kel* for one associated with "breaking." *Vin albastru* is blue wine in Rumanian.

SPECTRAL EMANATIONS

golden lamp: "Facing the table, near the south wall, stood a candelabrum (*lychnia*) of cast gold, hollow and of the weight of a hundred minae . . . It was made up of globules and lilies along with pomegranates and little bowls, num-bering 70 in all; of these it was composed from its single base right up to the top, having been made to consist of as many portions as are assigned to the planets with the sun . . . the seven lamps faced south-east . . ." Josephus, *An-tiquities* II, 144–7. Philo of Alexandria declared that the planets corresponded to the lamps in this wise:

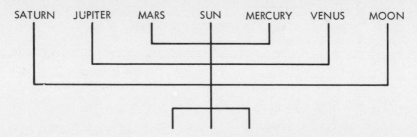

In the text of *Spectral Emanations,* Saturn and Mars have had to exchange their places. There are factorial seven $(7!) \div 10$, or 504, lines in the 7 sections of 72 lines each.

THE WAY TO THE THRONE ROOM   The original proem was "The Muse in the Monkey Tower" (q.v.); the present one was substituted part way through. The "bright river" is not Chebar, in *Ezekiel* 1:1; the ad hoc angels are named in various mixtures of Indo-European and Semitic. Roy G. Biv, who reappears in YELLOW, is the mnemonic acronym for the colors of our spectrum, and his sur-name in Hebrew means "sewer pipe".

RED   This is the westernmost branch; if such a light go out, the future will be ill (*Yoma* 39b). *A gourd:* the reluctant prophet Jonah sat under one (*Jonah* 4:6) to watch the destruction of Nineveh. The Book of Jonah is read in the synagogue on the afternoon of the Day of Atonement. ("Red" was started during the so-called Yom Kippur war of 1973.) *Parasangs:* Persian units of about 4 miles. *Adom:* like *Adam*, red or terracotta colored; the Hebrew letters that spell both words are derived from pictograms for "ox", "door" and "water".

ORANGE   *mere models of the immortal:* as the Mycenaean gold dug up, un-tarnished. *Gold is gold,* etc.: cf. *Pirke Aboth,* on exchanges. *The painter:* Philip Otto Runge.

YELLOW   *Queen of the Peaceful Day:* as Sabbath is supposed to descend on the lit candles on Friday evening as a queen of peace, so the secular sweet day to the daylight lamps of our eyes. *an anecdote:* an illustration of this scene would be a missing painting between *Consummation* and *Destruction* in Thomas Cole's *The Course of Empire* (1836), but the mistaking of Saturn for Mars is always more than a matter of the mechanics of vision. *Hilda:* in *The Marble Faun* of Haw-thorne, her copies of the Masters were more exuberant than the sleazy originals of her fellow-artists.

GREEN   *Man will nicht weiter*, etc.: Goethe, from the *Color Theory*, ¶801–2; he also observed that yellow was acidic and blue, basic, and adduced this scheme:

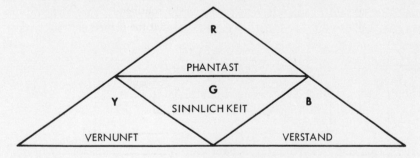

Der begrabene Leuchter: by Stefan Zweig. *Old guidebook:* presumably Haw-thorne used this. *seven-faceted stone:* cf. *Zechariah* 4. *Beatrice de Luna:* Doña Gracia Nasi (1510–69), born under her Christian name in Portugal; her story and that of her son-in-law, Joseph Nasi, later Duke of Naxos, are told by Cecil Roth in *The House of Nasi. A differently colored lustre:* cf. *Menahoth* 3.6 where the seven branches of the menorah impair each other's validity. *Vespasian's temple of Peace:* at least, according to Josephus, *Jewish Wars* VII, 148–50. *the earth has given its yield:* the end of Psalm 67 sung at the conclusion of the Sabbath on Saturday evening and reproduced, its text patterned in the form of a seven-branched lamp, as an amulet on the walls of oriental homes and houses of worship.

BLUE   *Day is naked:* cf. *"Le jour nu même dans ses nuances, ses nuages à genoux, ses ages, ses anges ingénus"* (Ephraim du Blé Engrenier). *No, green:* echoing R. Eliezer, *Berakoth 1.2. You had best build one:* this might be entitled "The Contraption".

INDIGO   *fragile virgin:* Astraea left us, to become a zodiacal constellation, after the Silver Age, which is why there is no justice in the world, but only in the stars.

VIOLET   This is the easternmost point; the labors of Hercules moved westward, hour by hour, but such a course cannot any longer be followed. *inside a pitcher:* according to Cecil Roth, some villagers in northern Portugal were still lighting candles in pitchers on Friday nights, a mere half-century ago, without knowing why they did so save that it was an old family custom. *Ten black drops:* the plagues against Egypt are counted out this way. *three higher colors:* as if the branches have all been lower emanations; there may be three higher ones, a source, a current, a sea, as oil streams into light. *cracked the oil:* "Light is like a niche in which is a lamp—the lamp encased in glass—the glass, as it were, a glistening star. From a blessed tree is it lighted, the olive neither of the East nor of the West, whose oil would well nigh shine out, even though fire touched it not. It is light upon light." *Koran,* Sura XXIV (tr. J. M. Rodwell)

ON THE CALENDAR   The month in question is October, 1929.

THE LADY OF THE CASTLE   Sheelah-na gig, a kind of obscene carving found on the walls of occasional churches and nunneries in France and Britain. Margaret Murray suggested that they might be instructive anatomical illustrations. The one I invoke is above the clock on the tower of Great Shelford church in Cambridgeshire.

AFTER AN OLD TEXT   Sappho 2; Catullus 51.

IN PLACE

THE WAY WE WALK NOW   This is perhaps about prose, as well as about life after verse. It introduces what start out to be stories, but get lost, amid other things, in the telling.

A WEEK IN THE COUNTRY   No ten days of story-telling here.

TRANSLATION FROM THE FRENCH   Theories of narrative are theories of nothing.

THE BOARD: NOT OUI-JA BUT NON-NEIN   *Oui* (French) + *Ja* (German) formed the original trade-mark of this parlor game.

CROCUS SOLUS   A single flower for Harry Mathews, Walter Abish and Raymond Roussel.

THE BOAT   The bed (with memories of *A Child's Garden of Verses*).

LIMPING ON LEMNOS, ON A HILL WITH WAVES   Hephaistos, flung from Olympus, hurt his foot when he landed on Lemnos.

A VIEW OF THE RUINS   Some readers may take this as the site of the philosophies (academics in the grove, peripatetics, dogged cynics, boring stoics, etc.).

MEMORIES OF THE GRAND TOUR   Whores used to—and perhaps still do—offer, for a special fee, "a trip around the world."

ASYLUM AVENUE   A poet walked to his office along this street in Hartford.

THE HEAD OF THE BED   *Epigraph:* This was a dream; I realized only after having written the 15 sections that follow that the two countries were called, in the language of one of them, sleep and waking. 4 *Vashti:* from the Book of Esther; *Orpah:* from the Book of Ruth; Martha: from the Gospels. 11 *Half his days:* from Sir Thomas Browne. 12 In folk tradition, the skies are supposed to open once a year on the festival of the Giving of the Law. The blind man is like Milton. 13 All these stars are visible in the August sky; before midnight, Cygnus and Lyra are together overhead as a re-collection of the dismembered Orpheus. 14 Chicken Little, in the children's tale, believed the sky was falling; *in vitro . . . in vivo:* as if tested in the lab only or on living subjects. 15 Harold Bloom suggested that the two female personages in this section were really the same. I am now inclined to agree.

THE SHADES   Windowshades, dark glasses, ghosts, degrees of color, shadows, and so forth. *traghetto:* a stand-up, ferry gondola across the Grand Canal.

TALES TOLD OF THE FATHERS   (THE GARDEN) Tiepolo gestures: the sun behaving like the 18th century Venetian painter of theatrical skies.

ROTATION OF CROPS   The title refers both to the method outlined in Part I of Kierkegaard's *Either/Or* and to the nursery rhyme about oats, peas, beans and barley.

THE ZIZ   This creature is very loosely adapted from the one described in Ginsberg's *Legends of the Jews,* Vol 1, involving also a deliberate mispronunciation of what, in the original, sounds more like "tsits". It is the poem's fancy that the phoenix exists today as the Van Allen belts. The names of the mythical commentators mean "eagle", "dove" and "rooster", in that order.

COHEN ON THE TELEPHONE   I have never actually heard the old phonograph record of the famous dialect-humor routine. The Hebrew phrase *bat-kol* (lit., "daughter of a voice") means an echo; the caller's son is Ben Cole because he changed his name from Cohen—an assimilated echo.

MOVIE-GOING   Written in 1960; time has revised the astronomy as much as the astrophilia, and Mars and Venus are no longer considered to be diachronic versions of Earth. In the *ubi sunt* catalogue of all the theatres that used to line Broadway from 59th to 110th street, I think that I mistakenly added a nonexistent "Alden" to the list.

ARISTOTLE TO PHYLLIS   The quotation from Wordsworth in the last line and the allusion to Aristotle's example of a sea-fight tomorrow were mostly for the benefit of a philosopher friend who had written on the subject of contrafactual conditionals in a controversy currently going on among analytic philosophers. I was also thinking throughout of Mallarmé's sonnet, *"Brise Marine,"* and the first line of my poem is a version of the French poem's opening: *Le chair est triste, hélas, et j'ai lu tous les livres.* Lines 6, 7, 9, and 10 of Mallarmé, as well as the title, are all echoed, purely with respect to sound, at various points. Aristotle's advice to the girl to get help in reading his letter to her is well taken.

HOBBES, 1651   adapts these lines from his own verse autobiography: *Frigus erat, nix alta, senex ego, ventus acerbus; / Vexat equus sternax et salebrosa via.*

FOR BOTH OF YOU   *tromba marina:* it was a sort of 17th century single-stringed bass viol; *Lares* and *Penates* were the Roman household gods.

THE GREAT BEAR   Nearly a decade after writing this I came across the following passage from the *Phainomena* of Aratus (fl. 270 B.C.) in re a number of unnamed stars (ll. 370–382):

> *For they're not arranged like parts of a perfect image*
> *Of something, as are the stars in constellations that move*
> *Along predictable paths as the cycles of time unroll*
> *—Stars that, in the old days, were treated together in figures*
> *Known by the name of what those figures most resembled.*
> *(Back then no one was skilled enough to notice single*
> *Stars, or give them names as individuals.)*
> *There are so many stars! Whirling about the sky*
> *In so many colors and varying degrees of brightness*
> *That ancient sky-watchers needed to notice them in groups,*
> *Patterned and figured together and glimmering into pictures;*
> *And thus the constellations were named, and never thereafter*
> *Could any star rise at night single, and marvellous.*

frigid conjecture: Baudelaire likens a cold woman to *"un astre inutile".* *any single sign* ... Wittgenstein, *Tractatus* 3.328 and, shortly thereafter, 1.0.

A NOTE ABOUT THE AUTHOR

John Hollander's first book of poems, A CRACKLING OF THORNS, *was chosen by W. H. Auden as the 1958 volume in the Yale Series of Younger Poets;* MOVIE-GOING AND OTHER POEMS *appeared in 1962,* VISIONS FROM THE RAMBLE *in 1965,* TYPES OF SHAPE *in 1969,* THE NIGHT MIRROR *in 1971,* TALES TOLD OF THE FATHERS *in 1975,* REFLECTIONS ON ESPIONAGE *in 1976,* SPECTRAL EMANATIONS *in 1978,* BLUE WINE *in 1979,* POWERS OF THIRTEEN *in 1983,* IN TIME AND PLACE *in 1986, and* HARP LAKE *in 1988. A new book,* TESSERAE AND OTHER POEMS *is published simultaneously with this volume. He has written four books of criticism,* THE UNTUNING OF THE SKY, VISION AND RESONANCE, RHYME'S REASON *and* THE FIGURE OF ECHO *and edited both* THE LAUREL BEN JONSON *and, with Harold Bloom,* THE WIND AND THE RAIN, *an anthology of verse for young people, an anthology of contemporary poetry,* POEMS OF OUR MOMENT *and was a co-editor of* THE OXFORD ANTHOLOGY OF ENGLISH LITERATURE. *He is the editor (with Anthony Hecht, with whom he shared the Bollingen Prize in Poetry in 1983) of* JIGGERY-POKERY: A COMPENDIUM OF DOUBLE DACTYLS. *Mr. Hollander attended Columbia and Indiana Universities, was a junior fellow of the Society of Fellows of Harvard University, and taught at Connecticut College and Yale, and was Professor of English at Hunter College and the Gaduate Center,* CUNY. *He is currently A. Bartlett Giamatti Professor of English at Yale. In 1990 he was made a Fellow of the MacArthur Foundation.*

A NOTE ON THE TYPE

This book was set on the Linotype in Granjon, a type named in compliment to Robert Granjon but neither a copy of a classic face nor an entirely original creation. George W. Jones based his designs on the type used by Claude Garamond (c. 1480–1561) in his beautiful French books. Granjon more closely resembles Garamond's own type than does any of the various modern types that bear his name.

Robert Granjon began his career as type cutter in 1523. The boldest and most original designer of his time, he was one of the first to practice the trade of type founder apart from that of printer. Between 1557 and 1562 Granjon printed about twenty books in types designed by himself, following, after the fashion, the cursive handwriting of the time. These types, usually known as *caractères de civilité*, he himself called *lettres françaises*, as especially appropriate to his own country.

Composition by Heritage Printers, Inc.,
Charlotte, North Carolina
Printing and binding by Fairfield Graphics,
Fairfield, Pennsylvania
Designed by Harry Ford